CW01023537

DISCOVERING LONDON

AN EXPLORER'S GUIDE

TRAVEL. DISCOVER. EXPLORE.

WORLD OF WUNDER

TABLE OF CONTENTS

INTRODUCTION

London always reminds me of a brain. It is similarly convoluted and circuitous. A lot of cities, especially American ones like New York and Chicago, are laid out in straight lines. Like the circuits on computer chips, there are a lot of right angles in cities like this. But London is a glorious mess.

— JAMES GEARY

Central London from above

Ah, London. Its busy streets are unmistakable. The melting pot of different cultures, beliefs, and even fashion sense. London is truly diverse at a time when we are striving for diversity and truly welcoming at a time when walls are being built and borders blocked.

As I am sure you have gathered, I bloody love London. I love everything about it, from the crammed tube, angry Londoners cursing a train delayed by no longer than a single minute, and the seemingly completely unpredictable and, at times, event-stopping weather.

I love it. The good and the bad, rain or shine, London is a city where people find themselves, carve out careers, and fall in love. It is my belief that once you have visited, you will love it too!

Now, I am getting ahead of myself, I know.

So, let's jump back, way back in fact, to a time when small tribes fished in the Thames, and there were no river tours in sight. It was in 43 A.D. when the Romans founded the city that we know now and dubbed it "Londinium."

Various sources include variations of the name used throughout history such as "Londinio," "Londoniniensi" and "Londiniensium" until the city was renamed "Augusta" around the year 368 to highlight it as an important imperial center.

The Anglo-Saxons would later establish a colony which sources from the 7th and 8th centuries called "Lundenwic," which translates as "London settlement or trading town." Then, in the year 886, Alfred the Great would proclaim the land inside the Roman walls as "Lundenburgh."

It was during this rejuvenation that records reveal the emergence of its modern name through incarnations such as "Lundin," "Londoun," "Lunden," and "Londen." Eventually, as we know, London was settled upon.

Not that London is always called London, as it has had a host of nicknames bestowed upon it throughout its decades of growth and rise to prominence in the world including:

- "The Big Smoke," "old smoke," or simply "the smoke." All of which relate to the dense fog and smog that the city was permeated with in ancient times.

- "The Great Wen." It was coined by William Cobbett in the 1820s, who "politely" compared the city's growth to a cyst or swelling.
- "The Swinging City." It was given to the city in the 1960s during the cultural revolution thanks to the growth of art, fashion, and music.
- "Where Royalty Lives." It was given to the city because of the residence of the British Monarchy.
- "Reykjavik." It was given to London by economists in 2008 after Iceland's banking system suffered a financial crisis, and London was revealed to be using the same system.
- "Home of Big Ben." This is self-explanatory, but London is indeed home to Big Ben, a bell hanging in the clock tower at the end of Westminster Palace.
- "London Town." It was coined by the song "A Nightingale Sang in Berkeley Square," which was made famous during World War II by Vera Lynn.
- "LDN." The city is also abbreviated as LDN for the purposes of marketing and social media posts by people looking to be a little trendier.

Right! So, we now know where London got its name and nicknames that you might hear it called, but that's not why you are really here, is it?

You are here because you want to know more, the nitty gritty; you want stones unturned and to be overwhelmed with so much information that when it is time for your own trip, you are a walking, talking encyclopedia with more dinner reservations, attraction tickets, and places to visit than you can handle.

Okay, that might be an exaggeration, or maybe for some of you, it isn't. Either way, what I can promise is that what you have in your hands will provide you with sufficient information to plan for, make the most of, and fall in love with London on your trip.

"How?!" I hear the naysayers cry, like Peter Moore (the official town crier of London for 31 years) in the middle of Covent Square!

By providing:

- accommodation advice
- food recommendations
- attraction information
- points of interest
- things for families
- things for couples
- things for individuals
- things for history buffs
- things for partygoers
- things for walkers
- things for transport takers

I think you get my point. You can consider this your essential resource for your next trip, and we will even include information on prices so that you can budget, too!

Let us dig in, shall we? But before you can even think about setting sail, taking flight, getting behind the wheel, or planning any kind of trip, let's get to know "The Big Smoke" in a little more depth, shall we?

1

WELCOME! BIENVENUE! WILLKOMMEN!

Where and what is London exactly? What makes it so special?

THE HISTORY

Before we look at the London that you will be presented with today, let's hop back a century or two in the DeLorean and look at the history of the now great city.

Founded by the Romans in 43 A.D., Londinium had a population of 50,000 when the Roman Empire fell in 476 A.D. Londinium declined due to repeated Anglo-Saxon invasions throughout the fifth century; despite this, during the eighth century, Londinium was named the capital of the Kingdom of Essex.

More Viking attacks followed in the ninth century, which led to the settlement of the Danish, who encouraged trade and started establishing business in the town that transformed Londinium into England's first urban center.

It was the growing wealth and power that would later attract King Alfred the Great and his Danish Great Heathen Army, who would capture the town in 886. It wasn't until 1066 that the Norman Invasion saw London conquered and the existing privileges, laws, and rights established by William Duke of Normandy. It was during this reign that the Tower of London was built, and London became England's capital.

A century later, in 1199, King John reinforced the self-government of the city, and by 1215, the city established the electing of a different mayor every year. The city was on the rise.

In fact, in the 14th century, London became a European hub for goods distribution, and its position only strengthened a century later, thanks to the textile industry. By the 16th century, London had over 100,000 inhabitants, which then climbed further to more than 500,000 by the mid-17th century.

Turbulent times were coming though, and in 1665, the Great Plague of London, which was exacerbated by poor living conditions, would kill 70,000 people, and just one year later, the city suffered the Great Fire of London, which left almost all the population homeless and burnt down most of the city.

London rebuilt. And boy, did they rebuild.

London reconstructed what is now known as "The City" over a 10-year period, including St. Paul's Cathedral and a whole host of museums, theaters, and palaces. When the Bank of England was established in 1694 as the second central bank in the world, it became the bedrock for the Empire's power and provided new financial flexibility.

The Industrial Revolution in 1760 was the next major step in the city's growth, drawing millions of people and expanding the city. Not without hiccups, of course, like the great stink of 1858, which saw the combination of the hottest months of the year plus the smell of sewage waste being dumped into the Thames causing the suspension of parliamentary sessions!

Things were moving in the right direction though with the population growing from over 700,000 in 1750 to over 4.5 million in 1901. By the end of the 19th century, London was well established as a major capital for finance and international trade.

In 1888, it was the extensive administrative needs of the city that necessitated the creation of a new autonomous territorial unit, the County of London, ruled by the "London County Council."

At that point, the country was split up into 29 different electoral units comprising the city and 28 other metropolitan boroughs. This led to an overflow that saw the population of the capital decline while the suburban areas around it grew steadily.

The London Government Act 1963 created "Greater London" and its own government structure within it. The divisions have since seen some tweaking, but the divisions made in 1963 are the very divisions that we see now in modern London which brings us to today.

MODERN DAY

Today London is both the capital and the biggest city in the United Kingdom. It is located on the River Thames in the southeast of England, at the head of an 80 km estuary that runs down into the North Sea. It has been a major settlement for two millennia and still retains its medieval boundaries!

To the west of the city, you will find the City of Westminster, which has hosted the national parliament and government for centuries, and the name "London" refers to the counties around that nucleus, too. These are split into Essex, Kent, Surrey, Hertfordshire, and Middlesex and make up "Greater London."

London is one of the world's "power cities," meaning it plays a major part in the global economic network. Making it no surprise that London exerts strong influences on the world's:

- arts
- entertainment
- commerce and finance
- fashion
- media
- health care
- education
- tourism
- transport and communications
- science and technology

In 2021, London's gross domestic product (GDP), which is a measure of the health and size of a country's economy, was a staggering 801.66 billion euros, making it Europe's biggest urban economy.

That is not all though. London also has the highest concentration of higher education institutions in Europe and boasts some of the world's highest-ranked academic institutions.

London is busy, really busy, with a population of 8,796,600 (*Demography*, 2021) that speak over 300 different languages (I told you London was diverse.)

It would be busy already without all of us tourists visiting, but we do, in droves! London is not only one of the most visited cities across Europe, with the number of visitors climbing to a whopping 44% between 2009 and 2017, but in 2019, tourists spent an absolutely mammoth $2.5 billion there (M., 2023).

Luckily, London is home to the world's busiest city airport system with 181 million passengers passing through London's six main airports in 2019 alone and Heathrow seeing over 5 million passengers a month as one of Europe's busiest airports.

In 2021, London was also the most visited city across the whole of the United Kingdom, with visitors then having the luxury of traveling on the London Underground, the world's oldest rapid transit system. (M., 2023).

The entire city is steeped in history and bursting at the seams with both historical landmarks and modern feats of engineering triumph.

The London Eye

QUICK FACTS AND TIDBITS

Before you start planning your own trip to London, let's look at 20 fun and interesting facts about it:

The Palace of Westminster and Big Ben

1. Those of you with a keen eye will have already noticed that Big Ben is not the name of the tower, or even the clock; it is the name of the tower's biggest bell.
2. Paddington contains two fake houses that were built to cover the metropolitan tube line.
3. Norway has gifted the Christmas Tree erected in Trafalgar Square every year since 1947 to repay the UK for their allegiance in World War II.

4. London is home to the Shard, the tallest building in the EU and the fifth tallest across Europe, with 72 floors and standing 310 meters tall.
5. The iconic red buses of London used to be multicolored hat just like the different colored routes on the tube map; buses used to be different colors to signify their route.
6. All of the banks in the City of London used to have to be located within a 10-minute walk of the Bank of England so that emergency meetings could be attended within half an hour, but the rule was revoked in 1980.
7. Waterloo is the city's busiest underground station, with 95 million passengers a year (Barnaby, 2019).
8. While we are on the subject, over half of the underground actually runs overground to allow old steam trains to vent steam.
9. Oh, and early plans for the underground did not include trains going over or underground; instead, they explored the viability of flooding the underground tunnels to create rivers that carried barges from stop to stop—I am serious.
10. Six and a half million people use a London bus every single day, which is half the total daily bus journeys in the whole of the UK.
11. London is visited by double the number of people that actually live there every year.
12. London University was the first in Britain to allow women to study and earn degrees.

13. Becoming a Black Cab driver requires up to three years of studying and requires them to know the streets of London like the back of their hands. So, if you are lost, find a cabbie.
14. It has been illegal to feed the pigeons in Trafalgar Square since 2003, so keep all those frozen peas to yourself.
15. London is home to the smallest statue in the world, "The Philpot Lane Mice," which is a statue of two mice fighting over a piece of cheese. It was created to remember two builders who fell to their deaths while arguing over a stolen sandwich. Who really stole it? You guessed it: A sneaky little mouse.
16. Over 80 billionaires call London home (or one of their homes at least), which is 80% of the total number of billionaires that live in the whole of the UK (*15 interesting facts*, 2019).
17. "The Statute forbidding Bearing of Armour" has made it illegal to don a suit of armor in the Houses of Parliament since 1313, so it is best you leave your suit of armor at home.
18. London was bombed for 57 consecutive nights during the Blitz.
19. London is the only city to have hosted the Olympic Games three times, playing host in 1908, 1948, and 2012.
20. Londoners love a drink so much that in 1743 they rioted in defense of cheap booze.

Okay, now that we know a little about London and some of the city's quirks and eccentricities, let's get to planning your trip. Grab your oyster card, a packed lunch, and some comfortable shoes if you are planning on riding the central line at rush hour.

2

PLANNING YOUR TRIP

In London, everyone is different, and that means anyone can fit in.

— PADDINGTON BEAR

London Underground Signage

This chapter will provide you with the toolkit to plan a memorable trip that exceeds all your expectations and will help you make the most out of every dollar you spend on your trip.

Before you even think about leaving the house though, the first question you should ask yourself is when you should go.

WHEN SHOULD I TRAVEL?

The time that you choose to travel will be impacted greatly by what you are planning on doing, so the first thing we will do is get an overview of weather patterns before looking at some key annual events that you might be interested in.

Remember though, every one of you reading this will have different interests, reasons for traveling, and budgets, so take the advice that works for you and toss what doesn't; it is your trip!

The best time to visit could be considered between March and May for two key reasons: the temperatures are nice and mild (making the underground much less sweaty), and the city's vast array of parks are blossoming and luscious green.

That isn't to say that late spring or summer should be discounted; just bear in mind that you will be traveling in what is considered prime tourist season, and both the hotels and airlines know it!

Those looking to save a little cash should look for deals in the fall and winter with the obvious caveat that it will be much colder; just don't leave it too close to December because London is truly magical around Christmas time—and the hotels and airlines are very much aware of that too.

Whenever you travel, expect two things: unpredictable weather and crowded streets filled with tourists, just like those who hopefully have a copy of this book under their arm.

Let us look at the average temperature and precipitation to help you make an educated guess about times to travel, but keep in mind that London is notorious for unexpected downpours and drastic changes in weather, so pack a coat and an umbrella just in case.

The average temperature and precipitation in London are:

Month	**Average temperature (F)**	**Average precipitation (in.)**
January	45/36.3	2.09
February	45.7/36.5	1.42
March	50.5/38.8	1.89
April	55.4/42.1	1.85
May	62.6/47.7	2.01

June	68.5/52.9	1.97
July	72.1/56.7	1.89
August	71.4/56.1	2.13
September	66.4/52.5	2.09
October	59.4/48	2.24
November	50.7/41.2	2.24
December	46.8/38.1	2.24

Next, we will look at some key events that take place throughout the year in England's capital to help you plan around things of particular interest or weigh your plans against the above weather information.

Regardless of when you go, it is vital that you book any events that you want to attend ahead of time, as tickets will go and places will sell out. The moment you see an event you like, write it down so that when you are done reading this guide, you can get booking and avoid any disappointment.

March–May

As mentioned earlier, for many the stretch between March and May may well be the sweet spot for seeing London, allowing you to visit parks and gardens as they blossom and enjoy cooler weather. However, this stretch will also be of particular interest to those who like the sound of the following activities.

Vault Festival

- **What is it?** The UK's leading independent showcase of artistic and live performance across theater, comedy, and other live entertainment.
- **Where is it?** Waterloo
- **How much is it?** $62.50 for a festival pass
- **Contact:**
- **Web:** https://vaultfestival.com
- **Instagram:** @vaultfestival

St Patrick's Day Festival and Parade

- **What is it?** A huge festival that features a parade and *a lot* of food and drink, showcasing the best of Irish culture.
- **Where is it?** Trafalgar Square
- **How much is it?** FREE
- **Contact:**
- **Web:** https://www.london.gov.uk/events/st-patricks-day-2024
- **Instagram:** @stpatsdayldn

The London Coffee Festival

- **What is it?** A coffee festival that features over 250 food and drink stalls, tastings, masterclasses, and workshops.
- **Where is it?** Shoreditch

- **How much is it?** $23 in advance or $38 at the door for standard admission
- **Contact:**
- **Web:** https://www.londoncoffeefestival.com/
- **Instagram:** @londoncoffeefestival

Gemini Boat Race

- **What is it?** One of the world's most famous and oldest (185 years old) amateur sporting events between the two greatest universities in the UK.
- **Where is it?** There are fan parks in both Fulham and Hammersmith.
- **How much is it?** Free
- **Contact:**
- **Web:** https://www.theboatrace.org/
- **Instagram:** @theboatraces

London Book Fair

- **What is it?** A global marketplace for the negotiation and sale of audio, television, print, and film content where attendees can learn the business and network with potential clients and collaborators.
- **Where is it?** Kensington
- **How much is it?** $81 for standard admission (although you will need to register your interest first)

- **Contact:**
- **Web:** https://www.londonbookfair.co.uk/
- **Instagram:** @londonbookfair

Hackney Moves Festival

- **What is it?** The UK's biggest outdoor fitness festival, spanning two days and featuring live entertainment and music, local food and drink, and running events.
- **Where is it?** Hackney
- **How much is it?** Free
- **Contact:**
- **Web:** https://www.hackneymoves.com/
- **Instagram:** @hackneymoves

RHS Chelsea Flower Show

- **What is it?** A flower show held by the Royal Horticultural Society across five days, it has been held since 1912 and is often attended by members of the British royal family.
- **Where is it?** Chelsea
- **How much is it?** From around $83 to $150 depending on which day you choose and whether you buy a half- or full-day ticket
- **Contact:**
- **Web:** https://www.rhs.org.uk/shows-events/rhs-chelsea-flower-show

- **Instagram:** @the_rhs

June–August

If traveling during the summer is more your thing, don't be fooled—make sure you still pack your umbrella. Oh, and expect the parks and gardens to be packed with people catching the sun and trying to eat their ice cream before it melts, too.

Notable annual events that you might be interested in:

Trooping the Color

- **What is it?** An annual display of pageantry that dates back to the 17th century to celebrate the official birthday of the Sovereign, carried out by their personal troops that include the Horse Guards Parade and the Household Division, with the Sovereign also attending to take the salute in person.
- **Where is it?** St. James's Park
- **How much is it?** Tickets are only available via online ballot. Alternatively, you could join the crowds on the edges of St. James's Park and try to get a good spot.
- **Contact:**
- **Web:** http://www.trooping-the-colour.co.uk/

London Pride

- **What is it?** The UK's biggest and most diverse festival that celebrates LGBTQ+ communities and includes conferences, theater shows, exhibitions, and tours.
- **Where is it?** Haymarket
- **How much is it?** Free
- **Contact:**
- **Web:** https://prideinlondon.org/
- **Instagram:** @pridelondon

Wimbledon

- **What is it?** It is the oldest and most prestigious tennis tournament in the world, bar none.
- **Where is it?** Wimbledon
- **How much is it?** From $100 to $325, depending on the day and court you want to attend.
- **Contact:**
- **Web:** https://www.wimbledon.com/
- **Instagram:** @wimbledon

Kaleidoscope Festival

- **What is it?** A scenic music festival that includes live performances, DJs, and comedy performers while offering panoramic views of the city.
- **Where is it?** Alexandra Park

- **How much?** $86
- **Contact:**
- **Web:** https://kaleidoscope-festival.com/
- **Instagram:** @kaleidoscope_festival

Underbelly Festival

- **What is it?** A pop-culture festival that offers live entertainment as well as food and drink stalls.
- **Where is it?** The festival takes place across two venues: Cavendish Square and Earls Court.
- **How much is it?** $27 to $54, depending on whether you are booking ahead or buying your ticket at the door.
- **Contact:**
- **Web:** https://www.underbellyfestival.com/
- **Instagram:** @underbellyfest

Notting Hill Carnival

- **What is it?** It is an annual Caribbean festival that's been a staple since 1966. Led by members of the British Caribbean community, it is one of the biggest street festivals in the world.
- **Where is it?** Notting Hill
- **How much is it?** Free
- **Contact:**
- **Web:** https://nhcarnival.org/
- **Instagram:** @nhcarnicalldn

September–November

Those of you looking to avoid some of the crowds will be disappointed. There is no avoiding them I am afraid, but traveling in the autumn will promise cooler temperatures and photogenic foliage for those of you big on sharing your travels with the world.

Photogenic foliage in the city center

The autumn also presents opportunities to really immerse yourself in the city's culture, with some of the annual events deeply rooted in England's history.

London Fashion Week

- **What is it?** A clothing trade show that is one of the "Big Four" fashion weeks alongside New York, Paris, and Milan, showcasing over 250 designers.
- **Where is it?** Charing Cross
- **How much is it?** $25 to $45, but demand is fierce, and events vary.
- **Contact:**
- **Web:** https://londonfashionweek.co.uk/
- **Instagram:** @londonfashionweek

London Marathon

- **What is it?** The second longest annual road race in the UK.
- **Where is it?** There are various spots where crowds will gather, but I recommend Tower Bridge.
- **How much is it?** Free
- **Contact:**
- **Web:** https://www.tcslondonmarathon.com/
- **Instagram:** @londonmarathon

Alexandra Palace Fireworks Festival

- **What is it?** London's biggest and best fireworks festival is held on Guy Fawkes Night.
- **Where is it?** Alexandra Palace

- **How much is it?** $20
- **Contact:**
- **Tel:** 020 8365 4343
- **Web:** https://www.alexandrapalace.com/
- **Instagram:** @yourallypally

Lord Mayor's Show

- **What is it?** A street parade that combines traditional British pageantry with carnival elements.
- **Where is it?** Throughout the entire city
- **How much is it?** Free
- **Contact:**
- **Web:** https://lordmayorsshow.london/
- **Instagram:** @lordmayorsshow

December–February

I can't stress enough just how fantastic London is at Christmas time, from the lights along Oxford Street to the frost on the Thames. It is wonderful, but it will be packed with holiday shoppers. But on the other side of that coin is the absolute buzz of excitement that fills the city that time of year. If you can afford the inflated holiday rates, it'll be worth it!

There will also be the opportunity to enjoy the following events.

Christmas at Kew

- **What is it?** A botanical garden packed with seasonal cheer, including sparkling lights, seasonal sounds, and Christmas trees drenched in color. It is magical!
- **Where is it?** Kew Gardens
- **How much is it?** $29 to $37, depending on peak times.
- **Contact:**
- **Tel:** 020 8332 5655
- **Web:** https://www.kew.org/
- **Instagram:** @kewgardens

Winter Wonderland

- **What is it?** A huge Christmas event that includes markets, rides, attractions, and live shows like a circus and an ice show.
- **Where is it?** Hyde Park
- **How much is it?** Entry is between $8 and $15, but attractions and shoes will cost extra.
- **Contact:**
- **Web:** https://hydeparkwinterwonderland.com
- **Instagram:** @hydeparkwinterwonderland

London New Year's Day Parade

- **What is it?** A two-mile parade that makes its way through West London and passes the biggest London attractions to see the new year in.
- **Where is it?** It starts at the Ritz Hotel and finishes at Parliament Square.
- **How much is it?** Between $6 and $60, depending on the kind of view you want.
- **Contact:**
- **Web:** https://lnydp.com/
- **Instagram:** @lnydp

As you can see, the price of the yearly events can vary, but pay close attention to just how many are free. This emphasizes the importance of planning ahead, because if you plan your trip right, it could be littered with free events that ensure you have a great time without a big price tag (keep an eye out for our free itineraries later on in this guide).

WHERE SHOULD I STAY?

Now that you have an idea of events you might want to attend and the type of weather you'd like to aim for (fingers crossed), it is important to consider where you will be staying. We will cover options that cater to all budgets, although London is an expensive city, so bear that in mind.

Budget-Friendly

We will start with some of the accommodations that will be the easiest on your bank balance, so you have more spare dollars to spend during your trip.

Park Grand, Paddington Court London

- **Where is it?** Park Grand, Paddington Court, London, 27 Devonshire Terrace London, W2 3DP, United Kingdom
- **Rate range:** $104–$167
- **Interesting fact:** There are also Park Grand hotels in Hyde Park, Lancaster Gate, Kensington, and Heathrow. So, if you like the sound of the hotel but the location isn't ideal, you can check those out, too.
- **Unique features:** Multilingual staff, USA, UK, and European plug adapters, umbrellas available upon request (one less thing to pack!).
- **Nearby attractions:** Hyde Park (Winter Wonderland), Kensington Palace, Serpentine Gallery

Travelodge, London City

- **Where is it?** 20 Middlesex Street, London E1 7EX England
- **Rate range:** $90–$112

- **Interesting fact:** This hotel was awarded a Travelers Choice Award by Tripadvisor due to receiving consistently positive reviews.
- **Unique features:** Breakfast buffet, taxi service, and 24-hour security
- **Nearby attractions:** Covent Garden, Coca-Cola London Eye

Travelodge London, Covent Garden

- **Where is it?** 10 Drury Lane High Holborn, London WC2B 5RE England
- **Rate range:** $115–$145
- **Interesting fact:** It is rated by Tripadvisor as "great for walkers" with a 100% rating, meaning there's plenty to do within walking distance.
- **Unique features:** Breakfast buffet, taxi service, and baggage storage
- **Nearby attractions:** Covent Garden, The British Museum, Comedy Carnival Covent Garden

K + K Hotel George

- **Where is it?** 1-15 Templeton Place Earls Court, Kensington, London SW5 9NB England
- **Rate range:** $140–$200
- **Interesting fact:** It is ranked as high as 72 on Tripadvisor's list of 1,210 hotels across London.

- **Unique features:** Fitness center, soundproof rooms, and conference facilities
- **Nearby attractions:** Victoria and Albert Museum, Natural History Museum, and Stamford Bridge (Chelsea FC's football stadium)

The Corner London City

- **Where is it?** 42, Adler Street, London E1 1EE England
- **Rate range:** $126–$154
- **Interesting fact:** It is the greenest hotel in London! Built with sustainability in mind, including water-saving showers and organic mattresses.
- **Unique features:** No two rooms are the same. They also provide bicycle rentals, and they are pet friendly.
- **Nearby attractions:** Various escape rooms, Whitechurch passage, and Stolen Space Gallery

Point A London Hotel, Canary Wharf

- **Where is it?** South Building, 21 Hertsmere Road West, London E14 4AS England
- **Rate range:** $80–$140
- **Interesting fact:** They value your peace so highly that some rooms are available without windows.

- **Unique features:** Blackout curtains, 24-hour express check-in and out, and baggage storage
- **Nearby attractions:** The O2 Arena, Museum of London Docklands, and Canary Wharf Tower

The President Hotel

- **Where is it?** 56-60 Guilford Street Bloomsbury, London WC1N 1DB England
- **Rate range:** $112–$173
- **Interesting fact:** The Beatles stayed here in the summer of 1963.
- **Unique features:** Car hire, breakfast buffet, and laundry service
- **Nearby attractions:** Russell Square, Grosvenor Casino, and Charles Dickens Museum

Ridgemount Hotel

- **Where is it?** 65-67 Gower Street, London WC1E 6HJ England
- **Rate range:** $112–$182
- **Interesting fact:** The hotel was named a Tripadvisor "Traveler's Choice" in 2023, rated as highly as number 68 among other London hotels.
- **Unique features:** Laundry service, baggage storage, and free Wi-Fi
- **Nearby attractions:** The British Museum, Grant Museum of Zoology, and The Cartoon Museum

CitizenM London Bankside

- **Where is it?** 20 Lavington Street, London SE1 0NZ England
- **Rate range:** $250–$260
- **Interesting fact:** The hotel utilizes an app that can make your stay completely contactless for those of you who are introverts.
- **Unique features:** A bedside tablet that controls the entire room, wall-to-wall beds, and a canteen that's open 24 hours a day for those who like a midnight snack.
- **Nearby attractions:** Shakespeare's Globe Theatre, Millennium Bridge, and Southwark

Luxury

If the above don't appeal to you, or you have cash to spend and are simply looking to stay somewhere a little more luxurious, you could also consider:

The Montcalm Royal London House

- **Where is it?** Royal London House 22-25 Finsbury Square, London EC2A 1DX England
- **Rate range:** $285–$386
- **Interesting fact:** Another hotel rated with a 100% rating as "great for walkers" by Tripadvisor.
- **Unique features:** A pool, soundproof rooms, and a rooftop terrace

- **Nearby attractions:** Enigma Quests, Bunhill fields, Wesley's Chapel, and Museum of Methodism

Shangri-La The Shard

- **Where is it?** 31 St Thomas Street, London SE1 9QU England
- **Rate range:** $977–$1,423
- **Interesting fact:** This is the nation's highest hotel and provides you with breathtaking panoramic views of the city.
- **Unique features:** Valet parking, spa and salon treatments, and a heated pool with a view of the city
- **Nearby attractions:** Borough Market, London Bridge, and HMS Belfast

Royal Lancaster London

- **Where is it?** Lancaster Terrace, London W2 2TY England
- **Rate range:** $284–$395
- **Interesting fact:** It is one of only a handful of hotels that are still independently owned in the city.
- **Unique features:** Spa services, shoeshine, and currency exchange

- **Nearby attractions:** Italian Gardens, Peter Pan statue, and Serpentine boating lake

The Chesterfield Mayfair

- **Where is it?** 35 Charles Street Mayfair, London W1J 5EB England
- **Rate range:** $329–$381
- **Interesting fact:** The site of the Chesterfield once formed part of the grounds of Berkley House, which was constructed by Lord Berkley, an English royalist soldier, diplomat, and politician.
- **Unique features:** Dry cleaning and ironing services, banquet room, and butler service
- **Nearby attractions:** Grosvenor Square, Hard Rock Cafe, and Park Lane

The Montague on the Gardens

- **Where is it?** 15 Montague Street, London WC1B 5BJ England
- **Rate range:** $294–$337
- **Interesting fact:** The hotel is based inside a beautiful Georgian townhouse.
- **Unique features:** Pet-friendly, special diet menus, and babysitting available
- **Nearby attractions:** The British Museum, Bloomsbury Square Garden, and Russell Square

The Bloomsbury Hotel

- **Where is it?** 16-22 Great Russell Street, London WC1B 3NN England
- **Rate range:** $383–$449
- **Interesting fact:** The Bloomsbury is an Edwin Lutyens' Grade 2 listed, neo-Georgian building.
- **Unique features:** Fitness center, bicycle rentals available, and a currency exchange
- **Nearby attractions:** Congress House, Soho Square Gardens, and Bedford Square Garden

St. James's Court, A Taj Hotel

- **Where is it?** 54 Buckingham Gate, London SW1E 6AF England
- **Rate range:** $298–$395
- **Interesting fact:** St. James's Court has a history that dates all the way back to the Tudor times when Lord Dacre, a treasurer to Queen Elizabeth I, drew up plans to build almshouses on the "Tothill Fields" of Westminster.
- **Unique features:** Currency exchange, spa and salon treatments, and butler service
- **Nearby attractions:** Buckingham Palace, Westminster Cathedral, and Victoria Palace Theatre

St. Ermin's Hotel, Autograph Collection

- **Where is it?** 2 Caxton Street Westminster, London SW1H 0QW England
- **Rate range:** $578–$647
- **Interesting fact:** This hotel is a Green Leaders "green partner," meaning they track their energy usage and follow green practices to protect the planet.
- **Unique features:** Ironing service, breakfast buffet, and currency exchange
- **Nearby attractions:** Westminster Abbey, The Guards Museum, and Palace of Westminster

Hilton London Bankside

- **Where is it?** 2-8 Great Suffolk Street, London SE1 0UG England
- **Rate range:** $377–$422
- **Interesting fact:** The Bankside is a historic building with a contemporary edge, located on the "Design Trail" in South Bank, every room boasts original artwork.
- **Unique features:** Indoor heated pool, bicycle rental service, and valet parking
- **Nearby attractions:** Shakespeare's Globe Theatre, Millennium Bridge, and Southwark

Sea Containers London

- **Where is it?** 20 Upper Ground, London SE1 9PD England
- **Rate range:** $359–$463
- **Interesting fact:** The hotel itself was designed by Design Research Studio and is set within the Sea Containers building that was designed by the acclaimed American architect Warren Platner.
- **Unique features:** Cinema, rooftop bar, and private balconies
- **Nearby attractions:** The Queen's Walk, Victoria Embankment Gardens, and Blackfriars Bridge

Quirky

Now for some quirky options for those of you who fancy trying something a little different during your trip.

Wombats Hostel London

- **Where is it?** 7 Dock Street, Tower Hamlets, London, E1 8LL, United Kingdom
- **Rate range:** $85–$162
- **Interesting fact:** The building is a former seaman's hostel that's been turned into a treasure trove for travelers.
- **Unique features:** A bar, courtyard, and private shower

- **Nearby attractions:** Tower of London, Tower Bridge, and St. Paul's Cathedral

Hostelle London

- **Where is it?** 458 Bethnal Green Rd, London E2 0EA
- **Rate range:** $127–$191
- **Interesting fact:** This hostel is for women only, so it is well worth considering if you are a woman traveling alone.
- **Unique features:** Pin-protected dorms, common area, and a kitchen
- **Nearby attractions:** Weavers fields, Shoreditch, and Victoria Park

Hostel One, Notting Hill

- **Where is it?** 63 Prince's Square, London, England
- **Rate range:** $67–$301
- **Interesting fact:** The staff at Hostel One are travelers too! They will cook you dinner and take you on adventures so they can share their knowledge with you and make sure you make the absolute most of your trip.
- **Unique features:** Free Wi-Fi, free linens, and luggage storage
- **Nearby attractions:** Kensington Gardens, Kensington Palace, and Hyde Park

Astor Museum Inn

- **Where is it?** 27 Montague Street, London WC1B 5BH
- **Rate range:** $171–$206
- **Interesting fact:** The Museum Inn is on the doorstep of the British Museum, so it could be a handy option for any museum buffs.
- **Unique features:** Free Wi-Fi, local discounts, and printing services
- **Nearby attractions:** British Museum, The British Library, and Bloomsbury Square Garden

Green Rooms London

- **Where is it?** 13-27 Station Road Wood Green, London, N22 6UW, United Kingdom
- **Rate range:** $23–$108
- **Interesting fact:** This hostel is aimed at artists and creatives, even providing discounts to them! It has no tellies (English for television) or phones and offers a peaceful space for creatives to do what they do best.
- **Unique features:** A garden, bar and restaurant, and an exhibition space
- **Nearby attractions:** British Museum, Madame Tussauds, and Tower of London

That should be enough options for you to find somewhere to rest in between all your sightseeing; now let's get into taking you around the city.

TRAVEL PASSES

For those traveling on public transport, there are two main types of tickets or passes offered to pay for your travel, depending on the length of your stay and what you are planning on seeing.

Both are available for purchase online at https://visitor-shop.tfl.gov.uk/en or physically at all underground stations, visitor centers, or at Oyster ticket stops in most London newsagents.

Travel Card

The London Travel Card allows you to pay for unlimited travel across your chosen zones, and you can pay for a day, a week, a month, or even a year.

The benefit of a travel card is that once you have paid, you no longer need to worry about adding money to it or getting caught short without enough credit to pay for your journey. You pay for your zones and duration and don't give it another thought. However, the price you pay will be affected by whether you want to travel at either peak or off-peak times.

Seven-day travel cards at peak time vary in price from $50–$90 and cover the underground, railway, and buses and offer a 33% discount on London River travel, giving you lots of flexibility.

If travel cards don't provide what you need, though, you could also consider the next option.

Oyster Card

Oyster cards are the most popular form of travel pass in London, allowing you to top up at any time and pay for single trips without a large outlay, and they can be used on all modes of public transport that we are about to cover in the next section.

Oyster card fares vary across the different zones, but are capped at the "best daily fare," which means you can travel as much as you like without worrying you are paying more than you should be.

For Londoners, the Oyster card is starting to die out a little in favor of contactless card payments, but that is not something I would recommend to overseas visitors due to the overseas transaction fees and charges.

Travel Card or Oyster Card?

Due to the nature of traveling overseas, your choice of a travel pass comes down to one important question: How long are you staying?

Visitor Oyster cards (bought online from overseas) don't let you load seven-day travel passes in the way that traditional cards do, meaning those staying for a week or two could save money with seven-day travel cards, whereas those staying for a day, or a weekend would save money by topping their Oyster up as they go.

For more information, visit

www. tfl.gov.uk/fares/how-to-pay-and-where-to-buy-tickets-and-oyster.

Oh, and here is another important question you need to ask yourself: How much walking are you planning on doing? Because if you are planning on walking or cycling, you could save even more money.

Next, we will look at the various travel options themselves to give you an idea of how you will be navigating the city.

TRANSPORTATION

Like most major cities, London has a plethora of ways for you to get yourself around. If you are visiting for the first time, I would recommend walking to get the full experience.

However, for those who aren't physically able to, or would rather reserve their energy between activities, or who just simply want to enjoy the transport options, you should consider the following modes.

The London Underground

Monument Underground station

The most popular mode of transport in the city covers all nine zones that London has to offer and will get you where you want to go as quickly and efficiently as possible. It is easy to use by purchasing yourself a "visitor

Oyster card," which you can top up with cash as you go and tap in and out of stations to start and end your journey.

Pricing is reasonable, too. Your Oyster card will let you enjoy unlimited trips within zones one and two (which is where the majority of tourist attractions are) for a maximum of $10.

The London Underground subway is very, very fast and offers multiple lines that cover the entire city and is always populated by friendly staff who know the underground lines like the back of their hands. The only downside, of course, is that while you are underground, you can't see what's above it.

Bus

This is where the big, red London buses come in.

A classic, big, red London bus

Buses are obviously much slower, but you are sightseeing, so what's the rush anyway? London is a beautiful city filled with landmarks on every corner, and traveling by bus will ensure you see the sights and take in the culture en route to your next adventure.

Bus fares start around $2 for a single trip, but you will need to keep that Oyster card topped up because they don't take cash.

Bus routes cover the whole city just like the tube, and run 24 hours a day, making them a very exciting option for those of you who want to sightsee on the way to sightseeing.

The number 9 (Trafalgar Square, Covent Garden, and Kensington Palace), 17 (Charles Dickens Museum, St. Paul's Cathedral, and the Monument to the Great Fire of London), 35 (Brixton and the Borough and Spitalfields Markets), and 139 (Abbey Road, Piccadilly Circus, and Trafalgar Square) bus routes are especially good for sightseeing.

Piccadilly Circus at night

Rail

Along with the option of going underground, you can also ride the train overground. London Overground trains cover a wide section of the city, including taking its passengers from central London to commuting towns outside of London like Ipswich, Reading, and Shenfield.

For some routes, when traveling through multiple zones, the Overground may be quicker than the Underground due to having fewer stops, and most will still accept your oyster card, too, so bear that in mind when on the move.

Black Cabs

The world-famous black cabs are famous for one reason: Those cabbies know where they are going!

It is a pricier option, but one that prevents you from having to navigate London's busy roads yourself and it still allows you to sightsee, and if you are lucky, you may enjoy an informative chat with one of the people that know London better than anyone.

Black cabs can be found everywhere, from airports to train stations and hotels, as well as being all around the city. Look for those with a lit "taxi" sign as they are free to be hailed.

As mentioned, this option is a pricier one. Black cabs are metered, and their fares vary based on the distance of your journey and the time of day that you are traveling.

There's a minimum fee of $4.50, although traveling just a mile will cost at least $8.50 anyway. You can pay with cash, debit, or credit card—no Oysters here.

Stay well clear of unlicensed cabs, though; not only are they illegal, but they could be dangerous. Always stay vigilant in your excitement and exercise common sense.

Uber is an option similar to black cabs that is also widely used across the city and can be used easily via their app making payment contactless and faster. Just bear in mind that London can be very busy at times, and I have spent a long time waiting for an Uber that was supposed to be around the corner but never arrived!

Boat

That's right: boat.

River Thames, riverboat service

London has a riverboat service that carries passengers across the center of London on the River Thames to 24 different piers (or stops). The boats even include a bar and an outside seating area so you can see the sights along the river.

It is my favorite way to travel, and I recommend that anyone staying in London travels on the riverboat from the embankment at night—beautiful!

Tram

London also has a tram network that connects the towns within south London, including Wimbledon, Croydon, and Bromley. Trams share their fares with buses, making them a cheap and efficient way to travel around South London; just don't expect to see them in the city center.

Bicycle

If you are determined to get your exercise in but walking is too slow, London is littered with docking stations (750 of them, to be precise) where you can rent a Santander Cycle (previously known as Boris Bikes) and enjoy unlimited 30-minute trips within 24 hours for just $2.75.

Bike rentals are easy, too. The stations accept card payments, or you can download the Transport for London app and pay for it there with your preferred payment method.

You could, of course, bring your own bike too.

Another one of my favorites is what's called "cycle rickshaws." They are essentially a bicycle with a seat attached to the back for two, usually pulsing with bright lights and sometimes even pumping music, too.

They are great fun and can be found across central London; just bear in mind that they have no fixed fare, and you will have to negotiate with the driver on price—keep in mind the physical effort they are about to exert ferrying you around!

They really are fun, though, and a great way to see the city's bright lights at night.

Cable Car

Another unique way to enjoy London while commuting from one place to another is the "IFS Cloud Cable Cars" which cross the River Thames between Greenwich Peninsula and the Royal Docks to provide stunning views of the Gherkin, Thames Barrier, St. Paul's Cathedral, Maritime Greenwich, and Queen Elizabeth Olympic Park. The cars themselves also include interactive experiences to teach passengers the rich history of London's Docklands.

Tickets are just $8 one way and $15.50 for a round trip, making the cable cars well worth experiencing!

Car

Those driving enthusiasts among you could always rent a car (or drive your own). Just bear in mind that renting a car will be very costly, and you will also have to find places to park along your journey, plus, the obvious of driving on the left side of the road, driving a manual transmission vehicle as automatic cars cost more to rent, the high price of petrol, and the awful traffic.

My advice would be to only drive if totally necessary and to leave your car wherever you are staying when venturing out.

PRACTICALITIES AND THINGS TO KNOW

- The national holidays are New Year's Day, Good Friday, the Early May Bank Holiday (which is the first Monday of May), Spring Bank Holiday, Summer Bank Holiday, Christmas Day, Boxing Day.
- Shop opening times are 9:30 a.m. to 6 p.m./8 p.m. Monday to Saturday, and 12 p.m. to 6 p.m. on Sunday.
- In the UK, they typically use imperial measuring systems, but they measure short distances in yards, feet, and inches, long distances in miles, the weight of objects in pounds and ounces, and the weight of people in stones and pounds.
- You will need GBP to spend in London which you can get via currency exchanges (which are everywhere), post offices (which are also everywhere and don't take a commission charge), or by withdrawing at an ATM if you are desperate—but try to avoid them due to expensive exchange fees.
- The following is considered basic etiquette in the UK: always say "please," don't ask about someone's weight, age, salary, or wealth, don't spit in public, wait in line patiently (that is a big one), and patiently wait to catch a waiter or service person's eye before nodding or raising your hand.

- London operates on two time zones: Greenwich Mean Time (GMT) in the months of January, February, March, November, and December, and British Summer Time (BST) during April, May, June, July, August, September, and October.
- The London telephone area code is 020.
- You can send letters, postcards, and packages, as well as exchange currency at the post office.
- The associated plug type in the UK is G; it has three rectangular pins positioned in a triangle. The UK operates on a 230V supply voltage and 50hz.
- UK clothing sizes are as follows: XS: fits US 4–6, S: 8–10, M: 12–14, L: 16–18, XL: 20–22, XXL: 24–26.
- All Transport for London toilets are free to use, but some non-tfl toilets may come with a small charge.
- Londoners drive on the left.
- Some words are pronounced differently, such as advertisement, bald, clique, either, and semi.
- Beer and cider are ordered by the pint, while spirits are ordered in either single measures of 25 ml or 35 ml or double measures of 50 ml.
- It is a common courtesy to tip in restaurants and cabs, but not mandatory.
- You should download Citymapper to help you if you are confused by all the different

transportation lines... https://citymap-
per.com/london?lang=en

Okay, I think we've covered all you need to know to plan your trip. Phew, the list is extensive, but you want to make the very most of your trip, don't you?

Next, we will explore one of my favorite pastimes—

Eating!

Let us tuck in.

3

GOOD GRUB

London boasts a wide range of top restaurants to cater to your needs, whether you want to get fancy with a little fine-dining in one of the 71 Michelin-starred restaurants, want a beer and a bite, or fancy an all-you-can-eat buffet to fill your boots before plowing forward.

London offers peaceful places, rowdy places, quiet places, loud places, veggie places, meaty places, and even one place where you eat in the dark. We're not talking about mood lighting. We are talking about a pitch-black room with visually impaired waiters guiding you through your meal. I tried it; it was weird, and apparently, chicken tastes much, much better when you can't see it (at least, I think it was chicken).

So, whether you are wanting an experience, a light lunch, or a three-course dinner, we are sure you will find something to suit your tastes with these recommendations.

Let us jump into some of the best grub London has to offer, starting with the crème de la crème.

MICHELIN-STARRED RESTAURANTS

Rather than doing a deep dive into all 71 restaurants (that would require its own book), we will provide you with a list of 25 of them, the type of cuisine they specialize in, and the area of London they reside in, in case you want to check them out.

1. Hélène Darroze at the Connaught, French cuisine, in Mayfair
2. Amaya, Indian cuisine, in Belgravia
3. Core by Clare Smyth, British cuisine, in Notting Hill
4. Sketch Lecture Room and Library, French cuisine, in Mayfair
5. Restaurant Gordon Ramsay, French cuisine, in Chelsea
6. Alain Duccase at the Dorchester, French cuisine, in Mayfair
7. Ikoyi, African cuisine, in Temple
8. The Clove Club, British cuisine, in Shoreditch
9. A Wong, Cantonese cuisine, in Victoria
10. La Dame de Pic London, French cuisine, in Tower Bridge
11. Da Terra Restaurant and Bar at Town Hall Hotel, Modern European cuisine, in Bethnal Green

12. Restaurant Story, British cuisine, in Tower Bridge
13. Kitchen Table, European cuisine, in Marylebone
14. Claude Bosi at Bibendum, French cuisine, in Chelsea
15. Dinner by Heston Blumenthal, British cuisine, in Belgravia
16. Le Gavroche, French cuisine, in Mayfair
17. Alex Dilling at Hotel Royal Cafe, European cuisine, in Piccadilly
18. The Ledbury, European cuisine, in Kensington
19. Cycene, Asian cuisine, in Shoreditch
20. Luca, Italian cuisine, in Clerkenwell
21. St.Barts, Continental cuisine, in Barbican
22. Taku, Japanese cuisine, in Soho
23. Jamavar, Indian cuisine, in Mayfair
24. KOL, Mexican cuisine, in Mayfair
25. Sollip, Korean cuisine, in Tower Bridge

Okay, now that you have a list of some of London's finest and most expensive restaurants, let's dive a little deeper into some other great restaurants that London has to offer.

THE BEST

We will include a key in this section that ranges from $ meaning the least expensive to $$$ for the most expensive to give you some context.

Mæne $$

- **What is it?** It is a modern British restaurant on the top floor of a four-story Victorian restaurant. It has massive windows, high ceilings, and exposed brickwork, making it feel informal, elegant, and relaxed. The menu is quietly confident and lets the produce do the talking. There's also a terrace for drinking and dining that opens in the summer; it is lovely.
- **Recommendations:** The gnocco fritto with iron cap squash and London stracciatella; snapery sourdough with whipped brown butter; Cornish sole with wild garlic; or the nutbourne tomato tart for vegetarians
- **Where is it?** 7-9 Fashion St, London E1 6PX
- **Contact:**
- **Tel:** 020 3011 1081
- **Web:** www.maenerestaurant.co.uk
- **Instagram:** @maene_restaurant

Paradise $$

- **What is it?** It is a contemporary Sri Lankan restaurant that packs some serious, serious heat. So much heat, in fact, that the menu warns you that "some of the dishes are very spicy," so no complaining! Those who don't mind the heat will be in heaven here, with the menu based on small, punchy plates of flavor and a small booth dining room to match with booths tucked along the wall and stools at the bar. It is intimate, clean, and very stylish.

- **Recommendations:** Stir-fried devilled prawns; slow-braised hogget shoulder roll with fermented chili; or grilled Ceylonese spiced prawn skewers with seaweed and kelp butter
- **Where is it?** 61 Rupert St, London W1D 7PW
- **Contact:**
- **Web:** www.paradisesoho.com/reservations
- **Instagram:** @paradisesoho

Needoo $

- **What is it?** Fun! Needoo is good old-fashioned fun. With Bollywood music pumping and displayed on big TV screens, Needoo provides a party-like atmosphere—and the food isn't bad either! With classic Punjabi cuisine that includes lamb, mutton, chicken, and prawns cooked on a smoky grill and sweet treats like kulfi to end your meal on a sweet note, your experience will be one that you won't forget in a hurry.
- **Recommendations:** Needoo's ever-changing dish of the day. If you have the choice, go on a Monday for the Karahi lamb chop masala or Friday for the King Prawn biryani.
- **Where is it?** 85-87 New Road, London, E1 1HH

- **Contact:**
- **Tel:** 020 7247 0648
- **Web:** www.needogrill.co.uk
- **Instagram:** @needogrill

Bentley's Oyster Bar and Grill $$$

- **What is it?** Aside from the obvious, it is a grill restaurant with a 100-year pedigree. It takes its history seriously, too, having retained most of the original features of the original building through its choice of fabrics, furnishings, and wallpaper. With American oak flooring and light wooden paneling, the grill is luxurious yet understated, with an air of calm. Bentleys even has its own bakery and patisserie.
- **Recommendations:** The fish pie is legendary! Stuffed with cod, smoked haddock, and prawns, it is served with a selection of seasonal vegetables and is *the* dish that you should have on your first visit.
- **Where is it?** 11-15 Swallow St, London W1B 4DG
- **Contact:**
- **Tel:** 020 7734 4756
- **Web:** www.bentleys.org
- **Instagram:** @bentleysoysterbar

The Clove Club $$$

- **What is it?** It is a modern British, relaxed, fine dining restaurant based in the Grade II listed Shoreditch town hall. Appearing regularly in "The World's 50 Best Restaurants" list and boasting two Michelin stars, this one's pricey but should be seriously considered if you are planning on splurging on one truly fine dining experience on your travels. The Clove Club serves a seasonal tasting menu and showcases dishes that are inspired by head chef Isaac McHale's own travels —which is pretty cool, too.
- **Recommendations:** No recommendations are necessary here; you simply choose from the tasting menu, the slightly cheaper, shorter tasting menu, or the vegetarian tasting menu and sit back and enjoy what comes your way.
- **Where is it?** Shoreditch Town Hall, 380 Old Street, London EC1V 9LT
- **Contact:**
- **Tel:** 020 7729 6496
- **Web:** thecloveclub.com
- **Instagram:** @thecloveclub

CHEAPER, YET JUST AS CHEERFUL

These restaurants promise delicious food at a fraction of the price for those looking to spend their money elsewhere.

Norman's Cafe

- **What is it?** It is a greasy spoon cafe that is quintessentially British. You can't come to London without visiting a classic British cafe and having a piping hot mug of tea after all. Even better, you will be able to get an entire meal with a cup of java for under $13.
- **Recommendations:** Baked beans on toast (don't knock it until you have tried it!) and a mug of tea.
- **Where is it?** 167 Junction Road, Tufnell Park, London, N19 5PZ
- **Contact:**
- **Web:** www.normanscafe.co.uk.
- **Instagram:** @normanscafelondon

Southampton Arms

- **What is it?** It is a good, hearty, British pub. Its sign reads *ale, cider, meat,* which probably tells you all you need to know. They offer bar snacks, meat, and booze. The atmosphere is as lively and jovial as you'd expect, and they only sell beer and cider from independent UK breweries.

- **Recommendations:** The hot roast pork bap—it costs less than $8.
- **where is it?** 139 Highgate Road, London, NW5 1LE
- **Contact:**
- **Web:** www.thesouthamptonarms.co.uk
- **X (previously known as Twitter):** @southamptonNW5

Randy's Wing Bar

- **What is it?** It is a former street-food vendor turned award-winning ranch-style wing bar. Its location is beautiful, too—right by the canal in Hackney Wick, and there are deckchairs to eat in when the sun's out. It is cheap and relaxing, but also very messy.
- **Recommendations:** Either the BBQ-slathered Kansas or sweet 'n' finger-licking sticky Korean-style wings—both of which cost just $8.50 for five wings.
- **Where is it?** 28 East Bay Lane, London E15 2GW
- **Contact:**
- **Tel:** 020 8555 5971
- **Web:** www.randyswingbar.co.uk
- **Instagram:** @randyswingbar

Bleecker

- **What is it?** It is an American-style burger joint that started out as a burger van before expanding to four London locations in Spitalfields, Westfields, Bloomberg, and Victoria (they also have a few delivery-only locations, too). Bleecker only sources rare-breed, grass-fed beef from small farms across the UK.
- **Recommendations:** No prizes for guessing this one: any burger. My favorite is the loaded bacon and cheese with a big dollop of ketchup. Prices for the burgers start at a fraction over $10, and fries can be added for another $5.
- **Where is it?** 16 Bloomberg Arcade, London EC4N 8AR
- **Contact:**
- **Tel:** 020 7929 3785
- **Web:** bleecker.co.uk
- **Instagram:** @bleeckerburger

Butchies

- **What is it?** It is a street-food stall turned restaurant that made its mark with New York-inspired fast-fried chicken before leveling up to a friendly restaurant with sharp decor. Its menu is as fun as its atmosphere, with names like "Jenny from the Block" (a chicken sandwich loaded with guacamole, chipotle mayo, and bacon) and "Cheesy Rider" (a chicken sandwich with cheese, pickles, and buffalo sauce).

- **Recommendations:** Start with a "Biggie" portion of the chicken tenders and get yourself some of "Butchies OG sauce," it is bloody good and will only set you back $15.
- **Where is it?** 22 Rivington St, London EC2A 3DY
- **Contact:**
- **Tel:** 020 3336 9371
- **Web:** butchies.co.uk
- **X:** @Butchies_London

QUIRKY

So, what if you want your food to be more of an experience or an activity, or an extension of all the wonderful adventures you are enjoying? Don't worry, we've got you covered, too. Forget fine dining or cheap and tasty eats; the following are restaurants that you will remember for way more than just the food.

Dans Le Noir?

- **What is it?** Here's a clue for you: *Dans le noir* translates to "in the dark." At Dans Le Noir, you eat in total darkness and are guided by visually impaired waiters, which is just as amazing as it sounds! You don't even choose specific dishes to ensure you don't know what you are eating until it is in your mouth. The theory here is that the lack of vision will only sharpen your other senses, such as taste, and add to the enjoyment of your meal.

- **Recommendations:** It is impossible to give a recommendation for Dans Le Noir, but you will be given the choice of either a red (meat), blue (fish), or vegan menu.
- **Where is it?** 69-73 St John Street, London EC1M 4AN
- **Contact:**
- **Tel:** 020 7253 1100
- **Web:** london.danslenoir.com
- **Instagram:** @danslenoirgroup

Bustronome

- **What is it?** It is a restaurant that is on a double-decker bus. Oh, and there's a glass roof to give you incredible views while you enjoy a six-course meal. This experience is truly one-of-a-kind and will allow you to combine your sightseeing with refueling. The journey begins and ends on the Victoria Embankment and includes Tower Bridge and Westminster Abbey.
- **Recommendations:** You will be choosing a set menu depending on how many courses you want and when you wish to travel, but I've heard from a

reliable source (my mom) that the panna cotta is delightful.

- **Where is it?** Coach bay, 40B, Victoria Embankment, London, WC2N 6PB.
- **Contact:**
- **Tel:** 020 3744 5554
- **Web:** www.bustronome.com
- **Instagram:** @bustronomelondon

Park Row

- **What is it?** It is a DC comics-themed restaurant and bar with live music and performances! Park Row was created to combine fine dining with fine storytelling and does so through five different bar/restaurant spaces that take its diners from the brightly lit streets of London to the darkest depths of Gotham.
- **Recommendations:** "The Joker's Grin" (beetroot gnocchi, salmon, mint courgettes, Mauritian curry, and lime leaf oil) or the "Big Belly Burger," which is made from "Wayne Estate Beef."
- **Where is it?** 77 Brewer St, London W1F 9ZN
- **Contact:**
- **Tel:** 020 3745 3431
- **Web:** parkrowlondon.co.uk
- **Instagram:** @parkrowlondon

Circus

- **What is it?** It is a Pan-Asian restaurant that also hosts circus entertainment and cabaret on a stage in the middle of it. We're talking fire-breathers, contortionists, and much more. Oh, and it is also a cocktail bar; how's that for dinner and a show?
- **Recommendations:** Angus filet steak—it'll cost you, but it comes with garlic chips, tender stem broccoli, and jasmine rice. If that's not enough for you, did I mention the fire breathers?
- **Where is it?** 27-29 Endell St, London WC2H 9BA
- **Contact:**
- **Tel:** 020 7420 9300
- **Web:** circus-london.co.uk
- **Instagram:** @circuslondon

The Clink

- **What is it?** It is a restaurant within Her Majesty's Prison Brixton with a wait staff made up of current inmates who are working toward qualifications in the food industry and rehabilitating themselves. It is a really cool concept, and the food is great, too. Just bear in mind that they can't serve alcohol, so mocktails will have to do.
- **Recommendations:** The heritage tomato tarte tatin with wild rocket and burrata is one of my

favorites, and if you are going for a mocktail, go for the rhubarb rose.

- **Where is it?** HMP Brixton, Jebb Ave, Brixton Hill, London SW2 5XF
- **Contact:**
- **Tel:** 02086789007
- **Web:** theclinkcharity.org
- **Instagram:** @theclinkrestaurant

BEST FOR VEGANS

London's diversity spreads to its choice of restaurant too, in which vegans and veggies are very well catered for. So well catered for, in fact, that in 2022, London was named the "most vegan-friendly city in the world" and boasts 400 vegan, or vegan-friendly, places to eat.

Tendril

- **What is it?** A restaurant that offers an almost entirely vegan menu. Tendril is dimly lit and romantic despite being just minutes from the hustle and bustle of Oxford Circus. If you are sick of looking for the (v) on the menu, you will feel right at home here as the tables are turned, with any dishes that aren't vegan marked as (nv)—not that many of the dishes aren't.
- **Recommendations:** The tiramisu—go try it and thank me later.

- **Where is it?** 5 Princes St, London W1B 2LQ
- **Contact:**
- **Web:** www.tendrilkitchen.co.uk
- **Instagram:** @tendril_kitchen

Tofu Vegan

- **What is it?** This place is like vegan heaven. Offering plates filled with mock meat, bean curd, and, of course, tofu. The entire menu is vegan, so there's no need to anxiously scan the menu; just sit back, choose your favorite dishes, and enjoy.
- **Recommendations:** Speaking of dishes, I'd recommend the "twice cooked 'fish,'" its batter is crisp, its 'fish' meltingly soft, and of course, it is vegan
- **Where is it?** 105 Upper St, London N1 1QN
- **Contact:**
- **Tel:** 020 7916 3304
- **Web:** www.tofuvegan.com
- **Instagram:** @tofuveganlondon

Club Mexicana

- **What is it?** "100% vegan, 100% bangin'." It is a vegan, Mexican restaurant that is hugely popular after starting at music festivals, pop-ups, and clubs. They serve burritos, tacos, and nachos within the hot-pink walls of a restaurant that really stands out from the crowd.

- **Recommendations:** The al pastor taco, totish taco, or the jackfruit "ribs" will hit the spot, but make sure you ask for extra guacamole if nachos are more your thing.
- **Where is it?** Kingly Court, London W1B 5PW
- **Contact:**
- **Tel:** 020 4516 1301
- **Web:** www.clubmexicana.com
- **Instagram:** @clubmexicana

Gauthier Soho

- **What is it?** Housed in a Georgian townhouse, Gauthier made the switch to fully vegan in 2021. The decor is understated, the atmosphere relaxed, and the cuisine quintessentially French. It's something a little quieter than Club Mexicana and more sophisticated than Tofu Vegan, but crucially, the entire menu is vegan here, too.
- **Recommendations:** The golden glazed swede with citrus marmalade and a miso-infused dressing or the roast fennel with pickled blackberry and borlotti beans are both winners.
- **Where is it?** 21 Romilly St, London W1D 5AF
- **Contact:**
- **Tel:** 020 7494 3111
- **Web:** www.gauthiersoho.co.uk

- **Instagram:** @gauthierinsoho

Purezza

- **What is it?** *Purezza* means "purity," which is exactly what's offered at the London outpost of the UK's original vegan pizzeria. Purezza is a modern and relaxed place to eat with all kinds of vegan-friendly toppings like rice-based mozzarella and wood-smoked tofu. If you are a pizza fan, you have found what's for dinner.
- **Recommendations:** Dough balls, mac 'n' cheese, parmigiana party pizza (topped with aubergine and mozzarella made from fermented brown rice milk, with nutritional yeast for a salty punch)—and don't forget Oreo pizza for dessert.
- **Where is it?** 45-47 Parkway, London NW1 7PN
- **Contact:**
- **Tel:** 02038840078
- **Web:** purezza.co.uk
- **Instagram:** @purezza

BEST FOR CELIACS (GLUTEN-FREE)

Celiac disease and the choice of eating wheat-free has risen exponentially over the last decade, so it is no surprise that London has a host of eats on offer whether you avoid gluten out of choice or necessity.

Andina Spitalfields

- **What is it?** A Peruvian restaurant with a menu that is entirely gluten-free— celiacs rejoice! Andina functions as a bar, too, and has two floors that include a basement dining room. The music is upbeat, the atmosphere lively, and the gluten nonexistent.
- **Recommendations:** The "cheeky ceviche" is made up of thin slices of cod cheeks and hake that are marinated in citrus juice with spring onion. Cancha, a Peruvian popcorn snack, is well worth a try, and you must try the pisco sour as it is Peru's national cocktail.
- **Where is it?** 60-62 Commercial St, London E1 6LT
- **Contact:**
- **Tel:** 020 3965 3482
- **Web:** andinalondon.com
- **Instagram:** @andinalondon

Indigo at One Aldwych

- **What is it?** A restaurant with a completely gluten-free a la carte menu that excludes dairy, too (bonus). Indigo is classy and clean-cut, overlooks the hotel bar, and is decorated with freshly cut flowers and a muted decor.

- **Recommendations:** The Cornish-tasting menu includes monkfish in seaweed and slow-cooked lamb breast; or why not try the gluten-free muffin for breakfast?
- **Where is it?** 1 Aldwych, London WC2B 4BZ
- **Contact:**
- **Tel:** 020 7300 0400
- **Web:** www.onealdwych.com
- **Instagram:** @onealdwychhotel

Niche

- **What is it?** A bistro restaurant that's entirely gluten-free and even has a section on its menu for those who suffer with irritable bowel syndrome (IBS), a condition commonly linked with coeliac disease—how thoughtful is that? It is modern British comfort food in a warm, contemporary setting.
- **Recommendations:** Both the Glamorgan potato cake and the chicken, wild mushroom, and tarragon pie provide the warm and fuzzies. Although, if you want something lighter, you might consider the winter kale super salad.
- **Where is it?** 197-199 Rosebery Ave, London EC1R 4TJ
- **Contact:**
- **Tel:** 020 7837 5048
- **Web:** www.nichefoodanddrink.com

- **Instagram:** @nicheglutenfreedining

Honest Burgers

- **What is it?** A burger chain with over 30 branches that has a menu that can tweak every single dish to be gluten-free—yes, that includes the buns, meaning there's no need to ask for a lettuce wrap. Honest Burgers is so committed to offering clean food that they have their own farm and butchery; now that's commitment.
- **Recommendations:** The "smashed burger" comes with American cheese, pickles, white onion, and brown butter mustard mayo.
- **Where is it?** 6 Bermondsey St, London SE1 2TF
- **Contact:**
- **Tel:** 020 3841 2330
- **Web:** www.honestburgers.co.uk
- **Instagram:** @honestburgers

Island Poke

- **What is it?** A health-conscious, Hawaiian-inspired restaurant that is almost completely gluten-free. The restaurant brings a South Pacific beach-shack vibe along with an R&B soundtrack. There are raw fish salad bowls to be eaten via a conveyor belt system, which starts with a choice of brown rice, sushi rice, or salad. It is great fun and provides a much lighter option than the sandwich that usually weighs heavy on you for the rest of the afternoon.

- **Recommendations:** Of the various house combinations to choose from, my favorite was the “ahi bowl,” consisting of sushi rice, marinated tuna shoyu, zingy pineapple, chili salsa, and shredded wakame seaweed.
- **Where is it?** 42 Great Eastern St, London EC2A 3EP
- **Contact:**
- **Tel:** 020 3982 0003
- **Web:** www.islandpoke.com
- **Instagram:** @islandpokeuk

Don’t forget to book ahead for restaurants that require it and always check the restaurants opening times online before visiting, no blaming World of Wunder when you are stuck outside with an empty stomach.

4

LONDON NEIGHBORHOODS

London is typically split between North, East, South, and West and made up of 32 distinct boroughs:

1. Wandsworth
2. Lambeth
3. Southwark
4. City of Westminster
5. Kensington and Chelsea
6. Hammersmith and Fulham
7. Hounslow
8. Richmond upon Thames
9. Kingston upon Thames
10. Tower Hamlets
11. Brent
12. Hackney
13. Islington
14. Camden

15. Ealing
16. Merton
17. Sutton
18. Croydon
19. Bromley
20. Lewisham
21. Greenwich
22. Bexley
23. Havering
24. Barking and Dagenham
25. Redbridge
26. Newham
27. Waltham Forest
28. Haringey
29. Enfield
30. Barnet
31. Harrow
32. Hillingdon

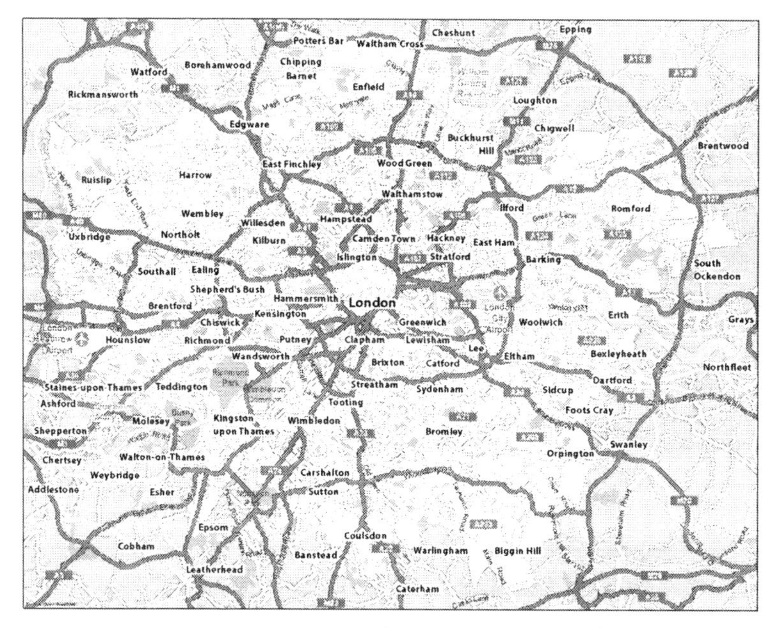

London Borough Map (Gisgeography.com 2023)

To download: https://gisgeography.com/london-map-england/#Reference

For additional downloadable maps, go to https://www.visitlondon.com/traveller-information/getting-around-london/london-maps-and-guides/free-london-travel-maps

Within those boroughs, there are a total of 48 neighborhoods. Still with me? Good, if you answered no, then keep reading anyway, and it will hopefully start to make sense.

Instead of looking at the boroughs specifically (some of them are big), we've picked out 25 of the most interesting neighborhoods to visit. We will also divide them between

North, East, South, West, and Central and indicate what borough they fall within.

Right! Let us start pounding the pavement, shall we?

NORTH

North London offers a unique mix of culture and a vibrant social scene. From quiet family neighborhoods and leafy greens to the hustle and bustle that London is known for, the North of the city caters to everyone. There's also a range of incomes here, with high-end and more budget-friendly neighborhoods, which only adds to how diverse the area is.

Hampstead

- **Borough:** Camden
- **Background:** Beginning as a Saxon village, for centuries Hampstead, or "Hamstede" as it was once known, was a quiet village where people grazed animals and grew crops.
- **Known for:** Green open spaces and a who's who of celebrities. Hampstead is one of the more desirable boroughs in the entire capital.
- **Things to do:** Visit the beautiful Hampstead Heath, have a pint at the Holly Bush, or snap a selfie at Kenwood House
- **Relevant links:**
- https://www.hampsteadheath.net/

- https://www.hollybushhampstead.co.uk/
- https://www.english-heritage.org.uk/visit/places/kenwood/
- **Hidden gem:** The Hill Garden and Pergola, a beautifully landscaped area that used to be the garden of a since-demolished manor house. There are fantastic views of Hampstead Heath and Hampstead Hill Gardens, so be sure to take a picnic.

Camden

New Rock leather and boot store in Camden

- **Borough:** Camden
- **Background:** Named after Charles Pratt, the first Earl Camden who began developing Camden Town in 1791. The earliest known settlement dates back to 7000 B.C.E. and was on the highlands of Hampstead Heath, with the area heavily forested for centuries.

- **Known for:** A sophisticated and diverse edge. Home to an expansive range of people and professions, such as bankers, bakers, lawyers, painters, pianists, and writers. The days of Camden being a hub for punks aren't too far behind us, and there's still an exciting music scene, but today, the community has evolved to include families and young children.
- **Things to do:** Visit the world-famous Camden Market, take a stroll through Regents Park, or take in the sights of Primrose Hill.
- **Relevant links:**
- https://www.camdenmarket.com/
- https://www.royalparks.org.uk/visit/parks/regents-park-primrose-hill#about
- https://www.thequeensprimrosehill.co.uk/
- **Hidden gem:** Camden beach! That's right, there's a beach in London. Well, kind of—150 tons of sand are used to create one every summer, so I suppose it is more of a "feach."

Canonbury

- **Borough:** Islington
- **Background:** Land in the area was granted to the Canons of St Bartholomew's Priory, Smithfield, back in 1253, and the area became known as Canonbury. Writers may well find inspiration here as in 1944 George Orwell moved to 27b

Canonbury Square, Evelyn Waugh lived at 17a Canonbury Square between 1928 and 1930, and Charles Dickens wrote *A Christmas Story* that featured the Canonbury Tower.

- **Known for:** Charming pubs from yesteryear, an alternative food scene, and beautiful Regency architecture.
- **Things to do:** Stroll down the New River Walk between St. Paul's Road and Canonbury Road, visit Canonbury Tower, and eat lunch at Canonbury Square.
- **Relevant links:**
- https://www.islington.gov.uk/physical-activity-parks-and-trees/parks-and-green-space/
- https://islingtonguidedwalks.com/our-walks/canonbury-tower-tours/
- https://www.goparks.london/park/canonbury-square/
- **Hidden gem:** The picturesque houses on Alwyne Villas, Alwyne Road, and Canonbury Grove.

Tottenham

- **Borough:** Haringey
- **Background:** There's been a settlement at Tottenham for over a thousand years, and it is believed to have been named after a farmer named Tota, whose hamlet was named in the *Domesday Book*. "Tota's Hamlet" and became Tottenham.

Side note: There is absolutely no relation between Tottenham Court Road and the neighborhood of Tottenham, which can be a little confusing.

- **Known for:** Being on the rise as a super-trendy neighborhood that's littered with art graduates, creatives, and anyone considered a little alternative. I believe the term is "hipsters," and they love this place.
- **Things to do:** Catch a festival at "The Drumsheds," take a taproom tour at one of Tottenham's many breweries or take a tour of the breathtaking Tottenham Hotspur Stadium.
- **Relevant links:**
- https://hypebeast.com/uk/search?s=drumsheds
- https://www.cktravels.com/best-tottenham-pubs-breweries-london/
- https://www.tottenhamhotspur.com/the-stadium/
- **Hidden gem:** Wander around the garbled houses of Tower Gardens Estate designed by William Edward Riley.

Primrose Hill

- **Borough:** Camden
- **Background:** Before the 1840s, Primrose Hill was wrongly categorized as a village despite having just one building, the Chalk Farm Tavern. In the 1840s, it was developed as a new London suburb,

with initial plans of detached and semi-detached villas with huge gardens. Some of those plans were realized, but London's rapid growth led to lots of terraced housing, too.

- **Known for:** Lush surroundings and some of the most expensive houses in London and filled with independent cafes, shops, and restaurants. Grand crescents hide colorful, vibrant homes, and the hill that the area sits on also offers stunning views of the city center.
- **Things to do:** Picnic at Primrose Hill and take in those views, stroll along Regent's Canal, or snap pictures of the colorful houses on Chalcot Crescent.
- **Relevant links:**
- https://www.thequeensprimrosehill.co.uk/
- https://canalrivertrust.org.uk/enjoy-the-waterways/canal-and-river-network/regents-canal
- https://www.allinlondon.co.uk/features/the-history-of-primrose-hill
- **Hidden gem:** Keep your eyes peeled for the blue plaques dotted around that signify some of the famous names that have lived in Primrose Hill through the years—if they aren't Instagram worthy, I don't know what is.

EAST

The East of London is the home of the docklands and a cultural melting pot that is just as famous for Brick Lane as it is for Jack the Ripper. Home of the Olympic Stadium as well as a host of independent art galleries and the infamous "cockneys" that are synonymous with British popular culture. There are plenty of tower blocks, and certain areas will have a grittier feel, but East London is on the rise, as evidenced by the recent investment in Stratford.

Dalston

- **Borough:** Hackney
- **Background:** Dalston derives from Deorlaf's tun (farm), and the first written record of the name is from 1294 as "Derleston." The area, which began as a hamlet on either side of Dalston Lane, started to urbanize, absorbing the surrounding areas of Newington, Shacklewell, and Kingsland to form one unified neighborhood.
- **Known for:** The best Turkish food in London, great boozers, and a beautiful independent cinema in a Grade II listed building. Known for its events, music, and nightlife, Dalston was named one of the "coolest neighborhoods in the world" by *Time Out* in 2021.

- **Things to do:** Catch a film at Rio Cinema, find out just how good the Turkish food is at Mangal 2, or take in some comedy or music at Evolutionary Arts Hackney (EartH).
- **Relevant links:**
- https://www.riocinema.org.uk/home
- https://www.mangal2.com/
- https://earthackney.co.uk/
- **Hidden gem:** Dalston Eastern Curve Garden

Shoreditch

Street art in Shoreditch

- **Borough:** Hackney
- **Background:** Shoreditch was notorious back in the Middle Ages thanks to the Augustinian Priory that was built near the "holy well" in 1158. The Priory spanned eight acres and was the richest nunnery in the country before being dissolved in 1539 due to the termination of the monasteries. Its name derives from the Saxon word "Soersditch" which is interpreted as "sewer ditch" in reference to the River Walbrook.
- **Known for:** Its heyday between the late '80s and early nineties, which saw the area rise as a creative playground with an equal amount of both grit and glitter. Now, Shoreditch is still known as "artsy"

and packed with cocktail bars and restaurants in the repurposed venues of yesteryear. A hotspot for bachelor, bachelorette, and Christmas parties.

- **Things to do:** Do a little vintage shopping down Brick Lane, catch a gig at Village Underground, an arts venue in a former warehouse that's under a railway arch, and be sure to check out all the street art, which is as free as it is beautiful.
- **Relevant links:**
- https://www.londonxlondon.com/brick-lane/
- https://www.villageunderground.co.uk/
- https://www.londonxlondon.com/street-art-in-shoreditch-free-tour/
- **Hidden gem:** Close-Up Cinema, a 40-seater independent cinema tucked away off Brick Lane.

Hackney Central

- **Borough:** Hackney
- **Background:** The name "Hackney" is a derivative of a 5th-century settlement that was known as "Haca's ey," meaning raised ground in marshland. The settlement was on higher ground near Hackney Brook and formed part of the manor of Stepney.
- **Known for:** Alternative nightlife, busy markets, and innovative dining. The area offers lots of fun and is growing as a new face of East London thanks to major landmarks and its transport hub

after previously being overshadowed by the likes of Dalston.

- **Things to do:** Sift through records at Atlantis Records, grab a cocktail that you won't forget at Happiness Forgets, or visit the Grade-II listed Tudor Manor, Manor House.
- **Relevant links:**
- http://atlantisrecords.co.uk/
- https://www.timeout.com/london/bars-and-pubs/hackney-bars
- https://collections.vam.ac.uk/item/O767721/the-old-manor-house-hackney-print-manson-john/
- **Hidden gem:** St Augustine's Tower, it is the oldest building in Hackney and can be found at the bottom of the Narroway.

Bethnal Green

- **Borough:** Tower Hamlets
- **Background:** Originally a hamlet in the 16th century, post-World War II, Bethnal Green shifted from farming to a working-class commuter belt. After the war, tightly packed streets were replaced by high-rise towers and greenery. Then, in the '50s and '60s, the area became the territory of the infamous Kray twins.
- **Known for:** Being one of the most vibrant neighborhoods in the East End. It is vibrant and has a rich history, with historic buildings and

expansive open green spaces. It is less busy than other areas and a little rougher around the edges than its East London neighbors, but it is still full of charm.

- **Things to do:** Reconnect with your inner child in the Museum of Childhood, enjoy a show at Bethnal Green's Working Men's Club, or take in the sights and smells of Columbia Road Flower Market (on Sundays).
- **Relevant links:**
- https://www.vam.ac.uk/young
- https://www.workersplaytime.net/
- https://columbiaroad.info/
- **Hidden gem:** Try to visit Wilton's Music Hall, the oldest grand music hall in the world.

Stoke Newington

- **Borough:** Hackney
- **Background:** Stoke Newington became a fashionable place to live in the 18th century after the wooden houses that perished in the Great Fire of London were replaced by those made of brick and stone. The idea of commuting, and the cleaner air that the distance from the city center promised, also played a part.
- **Known for:** Being village-like and quaint, Stoke Newington brings an element of peace that many other neighborhoods can't match. Church Street

is littered with cafes, florists, restaurants, and homeware stores, but the area never feels too busy or "Londony."

- **Things to do:** Take a wander around Abney Park Cemetery, one of the "magnificent seven" cemeteries of London, canoe, kayak, or sail at West Reservoir Water Sports Centre, or enjoy Indian food at one of the best Indian restaurants in the city: Rasa at Rasa.
- **Relevant links:**
- https://abneypark.org/
- https://www.better.org.uk/leisure-centre/london/hackney/west-reservoir-centre
- http://www.rasarestaurants.com/
- **Hidden gem:** Kiss the Blarney Stone at The Auld Shillelagh.

SOUTH

The South of London is slightly different than the North and East, being more of a collection of village-like areas that, combined with its urban areas, give a little taste of the best of both worlds. If you want a peaceful stroll, there are plenty of walks to offer. Want to do something more on the historic side? They've got that too.

Battersea

- **Borough:** Wandsworth
- **Background:** The name Battersea refers to the "gravel island" by the River Thames where the main arable field, manor house, and church were found. You have to hop all the way back to 693 to trace Battersea's governance; back then, the manor was held by the nunnery of St. Mary at Barking Abbey. It was after the Norman Conquest of 1066 that control of the manor was finally given to Westminster Abbey.
- **Known for:** Young families and growing transport links. In 2021, Battersea opened its own tube station as part of its redevelopment that included riverside restaurants, art murals, shopping, residential centers, and a swimming pool suspended between two towers. It is an area that is literally on the rise.
- **Things to do:** Catch a film underneath an old railway at the Archlight Cinema, hop aboard the Battersea Barge, or take a leisurely stroll in Battersea Park.
- **Relevant links:**
- https://www.thecinemainthepowerstation.com/
- https://www.batterseabarge.com/bbevents/
- https://enablelc.org/parks/battersea-park
- **Hidden gem:** Visit Lift 109 for a breathtaking view of London's skyline.

Camberwell

- **Borough:** Southwark
- **Background:** Camberwell was once an area that sustained itself with a mill and the surrounding fields; they evolved from sustainability to supplier and began trading fresh fruit, vegetables, and milk with London. The clean air and healthy water saw Camberwell become an exclusive Georgian retreat. Then, the construction of bridges over the Thames led to a new road network being built, and Camberwell evolved from a small farming community to an inner-city suburb of London.
- **Known for:** Camberwell College of Arts assures that the area is populated by artists and creative types for most of the year, but the area is also full of Georgian terraces and houses that have stood the test of time with freshly painted, bright front doors that catch the eye.
- **Things to do:** Take a stroll in Burgess Park and enjoy the view of the shard. Absorb some art at the South London Gallery or enjoy some smooth jazz at The Crypt.
- **Relevant links:**
- https://www.southwark.gov.uk/parks-and-open-spaces/parks/burgess-park
- https://www.southlondongallery.org/
- https://www.jazzlive.co.uk/

- **Hidden gem:** Enjoy some art, comedy, or theater at the 50-seater Blue Elephant Theater that's tucked off of Walworth Road.

Brixton

- **Borough:** Lambeth
- **Background:** Before the 19th century, Brixton was called "Brixistane" and is believed to have been named after Saxon Lord, Brihtsige, who erected a boundary stone at the top of Brixton Hill. Far from the urbanized version we see today, Brixton was mostly marshland.
- **Known for:** Its Caribbean roots. The area is down-to-earth, lively, and multicultural. With music venues, market stalls, and packed bars, Brixton is an exciting place to spend the day, but even more exciting in the evening.
- **Things to do:** Search for and snap the street art, wander Brixton Market, or dive deep into Brixton's heritage at the Black Cultural Archives.
- **Relevant links:**
- https://theculturetrip.com/europe/united-kingdom/england/london/articles/the-best-places-to-see-street-art-in-brixton
- https://www.londonperfect.com/plan-your-trip/things-to-see/markets/brixton-market.php
- https://blackculturalarchives.org/

- **Hidden gem:** Take a swim in the Lido, a swimming pool in Brockwell Park that was originally constructed in the 1930s.

Greenwich

- **Borough:** Greenwich
- **Background:** Greenwich has a rich maritime history, having given its name to Greenwich Mean Time and the Greenwich Meridian. In the 15th century, it became the site of the Palace of Placentia and was the birthplace of the infamous Tudors Elizabeth I and Henry VIII.
- **Known for:** Its scenic setting, museums, and World Heritage Site. Greenwich is steeped in culture and history, offering some of the most peaceful walks and serene sights in the city. The Greenwich Peninsula houses the O2 Arena and the cable cars that we mentioned earlier, too.
- **Things to do:** Climb aboard the historic Cutty Sark, visit the Royal Observatory, London's only planetarium, or visit the National Maritime Museum.
- **Relevant links:**
- https://www.rmg.co.uk/cutty-sark
- https://www.rmg.co.uk/royal-observatory
- https://www.rmg.co.uk/maritime-museum
- **Hidden gem:** Take a walk along the Greenwich foot tunnel.

Wimbledon

Wimbledon Tennis Tournament, center court

- **Borough:** Merton
- **Background:** Inhabited since at least the Iron Age. When the hill fort on Wimbledon Common was constructed, Wimbledon was included in the *Domesday Book* as part of the Manor of Mortlake. Its ownership has changed hands several times between wealthy families, leading to the construction of several majestic manor houses.
- **Known for:** Being a leafy, cosmopolitan, and vibrant suburb that is packed with famous attractions, including the incomparable Wimbledon Lawn Tennis Club. The city center is easily accessible from here, but Wimbledon is

interesting, too, with a host of supermarkets, boutiques, and a local library.

- **Things to do:** Enjoy one of the best walks in London at Wimbledon Common, visit Grade II listed Cannizzaro Park, or catch a show at New Wimbledon Theatre.
- **Relevant links:**
- https://www.wpcc.org.uk/
- https://cannizaropark.com/
- http://newwimbledontheatre.net/
- **Hidden gem:** Find peace at Buddhaadippadipa Temple just off Calonne Road.

WEST

West London is, for lack of a better phrase, "the posh bit." Encompassing the high-end luxury of Marylebone and Notting Hill, there's sophistication, there's luxury, and there are some of the nicest homes and hotels that I've ever seen. Expect beautiful, clean, classy streets that often have celebrities strolling around them.

Notting Hill

Hillgate Place, Notting Hill

- **Borough:** Kensington and Chelsea
- **Background:** In the 1800s, Notting Hill began transforming from an open countryside to a pig farming and pottery area under the development of James Ladbroke. James would develop a fashionable, cheaper alternative to Mayfair and Belgravia. In the 1900s, a lot of the big houses fell out of favor as people looked to downsize, and it was the large-scale Caribbean immigration of the 1950s that saw the big empty houses utilized for multiple occupancies that brought life back into the area, thus the Carnival's Caribbean roots.
- **Known for:** Being a cosmopolitan and multicultural area with terrace after terrace of

beautiful Victorian townhouses and high-end eating and shopping. This place is expensive, but it is beautiful too. Oh, and it is obviously known for its yearly carnival, which takes place in August, and that everyone should experience at least once.

- **Things to do:** Notting Hill Carnival—if your trip coincides, you simply must go! Shop for bric-a-brac at Portobello Road Market or take a stroll down St. Luke's Mews—it is one of London's most famous streets and was also used in the movie *Love Actually*!

Portobello Road Market bric-a-brac

- **Relevant links:**
- https://nhcarnival.org/

- https://www.portobelloroad.co.uk/the-market/
- https://www.globeguide.ca/why-st-lukes-mews-just-might-be-londons-cutest-street/
- **Hidden gem:** Visit the Churchill Arms in the summer.

Shepherd's Bush

- **Borough:** Hammersmith and Fulham
- **Background:** Shepherd's Bush was originally a pasture for shepherds en route to Smithfield Market. When the West London Railway opened in 1844, followed by the Metropolitan Railway in 1864, the residential development of the area commenced, including Shepherd's Bush Empire, where Charlie Chaplin performed.
- **Known for:** An absolute hive of activity that includes world-class experiences in music, sports, and shopping. Shepherd's Bush is old-school and edgier than posh neighbors like Holland Park and Notting Hill. The vibe is relaxed, the locals are young professionals, and the list of possible activities is lengthy.
- **Things to do:** Rock out at Shepherd's Bush Empire, roam Shepherd's Bush Market, or try your luck and apply for free tickets to attend a taping at the Television Centre.

- **Relevant links:**
- https://www.academymusicgroup.com/o2shepherdsbushempire/
- https://shepherdsbushmarket.org/
- https://televisioncentre.com/
- **Hidden gem:** Ginglik is a club tucked away underneath Shepherd's Bush Green that used to be a Victorian toilet.

Chelsea

- **Borough:** Kensington and Chelsea
- **Background:** The word "Chelsea" originates from the old English term for "landing place on the river for chalk or limestone." The first record of the Manor of Chelsea records that the governor of the King's Palace between 1042 and 1066, Thurstan, gifted the land to the Abbot and Convent of Westminster—what a bargain!
- **Known for:** Chelsea is iconic and filled with beautiful streets, plentiful shops, and cute cafes. Sophisticated, affluent, and very easy on the eye, Chelsea is one of London's wealthiest, most desirable, and safest neighborhoods.
- **Things to do:** Walk the Chelsea Embankment, stroll through Chelsea's Physic Garden (London's oldest botanical garden), or take a selfie or three with the Chelsea Art Club Murals.

- **Relevant links:**
- https://www.rbkc.gov.uk/parks-leisure-and-culture/parks/embankment-gardens
- https://www.chelseaphysicgarden.co.uk/
- https://chelseaartsclub.com/exhibitions/
- **Hidden gem:** The Ranelagh Gardens of the Royal Hospital.

Hammersmith

- **Borough:** Hammersmith and Fulham
- **Background:** Hammersmith's name was first recorded in 1294 when it was initially developing as a Saxon fishing village. A foreshore of gravel set Hammersmith apart from other parts of London that were mostly marshland and provided a rest spot for tired Londoners during the Middle Ages.
- **Known for:** Being a key London business district and home to headquarters for massive companies like Disney and UKTV. Hammersmith combines a busy town center, stunning riverside setting, eclectic shops and cafes, and a wide range of bars to great effect, but that's not all! Hammersmith also stands proudly at the forefront of London's art scene.
- **Things to do:** Catch a show at the Eventim Apollo or Lyric Hammersmith, check out the Hammersmith Bridge, or have a stroll in Ravenscourt Park.

- **Relevant links:**
- https://www.eventimapollo.com/
- https://www.lbhf.gov.uk/transport-and-roads/hammersmith-bridge
- https://www.lbhf.gov.uk/arts-and-parks/parks-and-open-spaces/ravenscourt-park
- **Hidden gem:** Furnivall Gardens is a beautiful park alongside the River Thames.

Chiswick

- **Borough:** Hounslow
- **Background:** Old Chiswick was originally an ancient parish in Middlesex County with an agrarian and fishing economy. During the Early Modern period, wealthy inhabitants built riverside houses on Chiswick Mall, and due to good communication with London, Chiswick was included in its suburban growth throughout the 19th and 20th centuries.
- **Known for:** Chiswick is an affluent area and former fishing village that offers many of the benefits of being a part of London without the hustle and bustle of it. The riverside community sits above the Thames and offers locals independent restaurants, upscale shops, and historic gardens and landmarks.
- **Things to do:** Visit Chiswick House and Gardens, an 18th-century Palladian villa, take a long stroll

down Strand on the Green, and soak in the sun and the history of Gunnersbury Park.

- **Relevant links:**
- https://chiswickhouseandgardens.org.uk/
- https://chiswickcalendar.co.uk/this-is-chiswick/places/strand-on-the-green/
- https://www.visitgunnersbury.org/
- **Hidden gem:** Ride a Santander Cycle along the cycle path from Chiswick to Richmond.

CENTRAL

Realistically, this is where you will spend most of your time. The center of London is its beating heart, packed with tourist attractions, busy shops, and over-booked restaurants. An eclectic mix of culture, commerce, innovation, and, of course, tradition. This is where you will find all the big-hitter attractions like the British Museum, London Eye, and Westminster Abbey.

Mayfair

- **Borough:** City of Westminster
- **Background:** Originally, Mayfair was part of the Manor of Eia and mostly rural until the early 18th century. Its reputation initially grew because of the growing popularity of the annual May Fair between 1686 and 1764. However, when the fair started to become a public nuisance, the future

Dukes of Westminster, the Grosvenor family, acquired it through marriage and began to develop Berkeley Square, Grosvenor Square, and Hanover Square under Thomas Barlow's direction.

- **Known for:** Being one of the most expensive neighborhoods anywhere in the world. Packed with elegant Edwardian apartment buildings, lush 18th-century mansions, and shops, you will need to remortgage your house to buy anything in.
- **Things to do:** Become awestruck by the artwork in Apsley House, tiptoe around the pristine lawns of Grosvenor Square, and take in the world-class exhibitions of the Royal Academy of Arts.
- **Relevant links:**
- https://www.english-heritage.org.uk/visit/places/apsley-house/
- https://www.grosvenorsquare.org/
- https://www.royalacademy.org.uk/
- **Hidden gem:** There are more blue plaques to find here too signifying places where famous stars have lived or worked (I won't spoil anything, just go look).

Covent Garden

Covent Garden Market

- **Borough:** Camden
- **Background:** We must travel all the way back to 1200 to find the first record of Covent Garden, when it was owned by Westminster Abbey and consisted of fields that included "the garden of Abbey and Convent," which explains the name. The land was then granted to John Russell, 1st Earl of Bedford, in 1540, and his descendent, King Charles I, the 5th Earl of Bedford, transformed it into the country's first public square a decade later.
- **Known for:** Being a world-class dining and shopping hub in the heart of London. It is always buzzing with excited shoppers crowded around

street performers, taking in a show, or enjoying some of the food on offer.

- **Things to do:** Explore Covent Garden Market, head to the Royal Opera House for a night of ballet or opera, or transport yourself back in time at the London Transport Museum.
- **Relevant links:**
- https://www.coventgarden.london
- https://www.roh.org.uk/
- https://www.ltmuseum.co.uk/
- **Hidden gem:** Stroll through Cecil Court between St. Martin's Lane and Charing Cross road for a slice of 17th Century London.

Soho

- **Borough:** City of Westminster
- **Background:** "Soho!" With a name that derives from a hunting cry, it is no surprise that Soho was an area of farmlands in the Middle Ages before it was acquired by the crown in the 1530s. Its later development was at the hands of Gregory King, an urban developer from the 17th century.
- **Known for:** Being the city's main entertainment district and London's beating heart, it is absolutely packed with bars, nightclubs, theaters, restaurants, cafes, and a little adult entertainment. It only gets livelier at night, too.

- **Things to do:** Take a stroll down Carnaby Street, go shopping on Oxford and Regent Street, or catch a show at the legendary Prince Edward Theater.
- **Relevant links:**
- https://www.carnaby.co.uk/
- https://www.oxfordstreet.co.uk/
- https://www.princeedwardtheatre.co.uk/
- **Hidden gem:** Hunt for the "seven noses of Soho."

Highgate

- **Borough:** Camden
- **Background:** Highgate was a distinct village located just outside of London until late Victorian times before joining the Bishop of London's hunting estate. It was those hunting grounds that inspired its name due to a high hedge that surrounded the estate. What was seen as "the gate in the hedge" became the name Highgate.
- **Known for:** Being expensive, one of the most expensive neighborhoods in London, in fact. It also has three active conservation organizations: Highgate Conservation, The Highgate Neighborhood Forum, and the Highgate Society. Highgate village is lined with Georgian architecture and littered with elegant landmarks, including the Victorian Highgate Cemetery, which is where philosopher Karl Marx was laid to rest.

- **Things to do:** Pay your respects at Highgate Cemetery, peer through the gates of the Victorian, neo-Gothic Holly Village, or take a walk and breathe in lungfuls of fresh air at Hampstead Heath.
- **Relevant links:**
- https://highgatecemetery.org/
- https://www.londonxlondon.com/holly-village/
- https://www.hampsteadheath.net/
- **Hidden gem:** There are more blue plaques to be found here—including Charles Dickens.

Bloomsbury

- **Borough:** Camden
- **Background:** Bloomsbury has been dominated for centuries by two iconic institutions, the British Museum, which was built in 1753, and the University of London, which was built in 1836. Unsurprisingly, it has a reputation as being an intellectual little slice of London, which is given even more credence by the fact that its former residents include T.S. Eliot, Virginia Woolf, and Charles Dickens.
- **Known for:** Picturesque Georgian squares with the perks of village life. A gathering place for young creatives, with roots in fashion, art, and, of course, literature. Bloomsbury also offers rows of high-end shops and restaurants.

- **Things to do:** Be transported back in time by the British Museum, wander down Woburn Walk, a Georgian street designed back in 1822 that was London's first ever pedestrian shopping street, or grab a bite from the cafe in Russell Square Gardens.
- **Relevant links:**
- https://www.britishmuseum.org
- https://www.ianvisits.co.uk/articles/londons-alleys-woburn-walk-wc1-29531/
- https://caffetropea.co.uk/
- **Hidden gem:** Find peace and tranquility and take in the views from the Japanese roof garden on top of the SOAS University of London.

Next, we will explore some of the attractions that can be found in not only these neighborhoods, but the city as a whole.

A LITTLE-KNOWN GEM

"I've been walking about London for the last 30 years, and I find something fresh in it every day."

— *WALTER BESANT*

For an unforgettable extra that will give you a unique insight into London, visit the house and museum of the great English architect Sir John Soan.

Soan built the house himself two centuries ago and not only lived there but also used it to house his vast collection of wonders. The museum has been preserved since his death in 1837 and offers a spectacular array of antiques, sculptures, paintings, and architectural models—a feast for the eyes and a little-known gem hidden in the heart of London.

You'll find the museum at 13 Lincoln's Inn Fields, London, WC2A 3BP, and a self-guided walk around the house is absolutely free. They're only open between Wednesday and Sunday, though, so plan your trip carefully.

Many travelers miss out on unique experiences like this because they're the ones the guidebooks leave out. You can help ensure Soan's vast collection gets the attention it deserves.

By leaving a review of this book on Amazon, you'll point fellow travelers looking for a true taste of London in the direction of the sort of travel guide they crave.

Simply by leaving a short review and a little about what you've found here, you'll help other travelers make the most of their visit and ensure important figures like Sir John Soan get the attention they deserve, too!

Thank you so much for your support, and enjoy your visit! It truly is an experience.

5

MUST-VISIT ATTRACTIONS

London is bursting with attractions, activities, and things to do, many of which we've already touched upon. In this chapter, we will explore theaters, museums, casinos, and much, much more! So, whether you are alone, with your family, looking to spend a little cash or spend nothing at all, looking for peaceful sightseeing tours or action-packed adventures, we've got you covered.

Disclaimer: The theater in London is some of the best on the planet and should be the attention of at least one of your evenings, if not two. Tickets can be purchased in advance at https://www.london-theater-tickets.com or you can visit the TKTS booth in Leicester Square that offers increasingly discounted tickets the closer it gets to show time!

Right, let's carry on, shall we?

FREE

Museums

British Museum

- **What is it?** It is a public museum dedicated to documenting the story of human culture and history through art.
- **Where is it?** Great Russell St, London WC1B 3DG
- **When to visit?** Late afternoon on weekdays
- **Nearest tube station:** Tottenham Court Road
- **Interesting fact:** It has the largest permanent collection in the world with eight million different works.
- **Contact:**
- **Tel:** 020 7323 8000
- **Web:** www.britishmuseum.org
- **Instagram:** @britishmuseum

Victoria and Albert Museum

- **What is it?** It is the world's biggest museum dedicated to applied arts and decorative art and design.
- **Where is it?** Cromwell Rd, London SW7 2RL
- **When to visit?** Thursday afternoons
- **Nearest tube station:** South Kensington Station

- **Interesting fact:** It was named after Queen Victoria and Prince Albert when it was founded in 1852.
- **Contact:**
- **Tel:** 020 7942 2000
- **Web:** www.vam.ac.uk
- **Instagram:** @vamuseum

Natural History Museum

The Natural History Museum

- **What is it?** It is a world-class museum and science research center that tackles some of the world's biggest challenges.
- **Where is it?** The Natural History Museum, Cromwell Rd, South Kensington, London SW7 5BD

- **When to visit?** Wednesday and Thursday after 3 p.m.
- **Nearest tube station:** South Kensington Station
- **Interesting fact:** The word "dinosaur" was invented by the founder of the museum, Richard Owen.
- **Contact:**
- **Tel:** 020 7942 5000
- **Web:** www.nhm.ac.uk
- **Instagram:** @natural_history_museum

Queen's House

- **What is it?** It is a former royal residence built between 1616 and 1635 that is now an open treasure trove of art, craft, creativity, and design for the public to explore.
- **Where is it?** Romney Rd, London SE10 9NF
- **When to visit?** Weekdays
- **Nearest tube station:** Cutty Sark
- **Interesting fact:** Queen's House was the first fully Classical building in England.
- **Contact:**
- **Tel:** 020 8312 6608
- **Web:** www.rmg.co.uk
- **Instagram:** @royalmuseumsgreenwich

London Mithraeum

- **What is it?** It is a Roman Mithraeum that was discovered during the construction of a building in 1954, now showcasing Roman artifacts.
- **Where is it?** 12 Walbrook, London EC4N 8AA
- **When to visit?** Weekdays after 3 p.m.
- **Nearest tube station:** Bank
- **Interesting fact:** It is London's smallest museum.
- **Contact:**
- **Web:** www.londonmithraeum.com

Imperial War Museum

- **What is it?** It is a collection of recreated World War I trenches, Blitz reenactments, and revolving military exhibitions.
- **Where is it?** Lambeth Rd, London SE1 6HZ
- **When to visit?** Weekdays between 10 a.m. and 12 p.m.
- **Nearest tube station:** Lambeth North
- **Interesting fact:** The museum was established in 1917 during World War I.
- **Contact:**
- **Tel:** 020 7416 5000
- **Web:** www.iwm.org.uk
- **Instagram:** @imperialwarmuseums

National Maritime Museum

- **What is it?** It is a celebration of the UK's maritime history.
- **Where is it?** Romney Rd, London SE10 9NF
- **When to visit?** November or December outside of the holiday periods
- **Nearest tube station:** Cutty Sark
- **Interesting fact:** The "abolition of the slave trade" medal is on display here.
- **Contact:**
- **Tel:** 020 8312 6608
- **Web:** www.rmg.co.uk
- **Instagram:** @royalmusuemsgreenwich

Science Museum

- **What is it?** It is Europe's most popular science and technology museum, with over 15,000 unique objects on display, ever-changing interactive exhibits, and a 3D simulator.
- **Where is it?** Exhibition Rd, South Kensington, London SW7 2DD
- **When to visit?** Tuesday or Thursday as it opens
- **Nearest tube station:** South Kensington
- **Interesting fact:** The museum's early exhibitions highlighted environmental issues like smoke pollution, which might not sound that impressive

now, but it was way ahead of its time back in the 1930s.

- **Contact:**
- **Tel:** 0330 058 0058
- **Web:** www.sciencemuseum.org.uk
- **Instagram:** @sciencemuseum

Horniman Museum and Gardens

- **What is it?** It is a quirky museum with displays of anthropology, taxidermy animals, and musical instruments.
- **Where is it?** 100 London Rd, London SE23 3PQ
- **When to visit?** Early on a weekday
- **Nearest tube station:** Forest Hill Station
- **Interesting fact:** The museum contains a living rainforest display where you can see tropical butterflies.
- **Contact:**
- **Tel:** 020 8699 1872
- **Web:** www.horniman.ac.uk

Museum of London Docklands

- **What is it?** It is a museum that details the growth of the Port of London, the rich history of the River Thames, and the link between the Atlantic slave trade and London's docks.

- **Where is it?** No 1, West India Quay, Hertsmere Rd, London E14 4AL
- **When to visit?** Weekdays after 3 p.m.
- **Nearest tube station:** Westferry
- **Interesting fact:** The museum itself is based inside a warehouse that's over 200 years old.
- **Contact:**
- **Tel:** 020 7001 9844
- **Web:** www.museumoflondon.org.uk
- **Instagram:** @museumoflondon

Art Galleries

Tate Modern

- **What is it?** It is an iconic art gallery housing the UK's collection of contemporary and international art.
- **Where is it?** Bankside, London SE1 9TG
- **When to visit?** Between October and March, so you can catch the installations hosted by Turbine Hall.
- **Nearest tube station:** Blackfriars
- **Interesting fact:** The Tate Modern used to be the Bankside Power Station, which was designed by the same architect that devised London's iconic red telephone boxes, Giles Gilbert Scott.
- **Contact:**
- **Tel:** 020 7887 8888

- **Web:** www.tate.org.uk
- **Instagram:** @tate

Royal Academy of Arts

- **What is it?** It is an independent and privately funded art institution where art has been made, exhibited, and debated since 1768.
- **Where is it?** Burlington House, Piccadilly, London W1J 0BD
- **When to visit?** Weekday mornings as early as possible
- **Nearest tube station:** Green Park
- **Interesting fact:** The academy is Britain's oldest art school.
- **Contact:**
- **Tel:** 020 7300 8090
- **Web:** www.royalacademy.org.uk
- **Instagram:** @royalacademyarts

National Gallery

- **What is it?** It is home to one of the greatest collections of paintings in the world, with 2,300 paintings that date from the mid-13th century up to the 1900s.
- **Where is it?** Trafalgar Square, London WC2N 5DN
- **When to visit?** Early mornings on weekdays

- **Nearest tube station:** Leicester Square
- **Interesting fact:** When the gallery was originally established in 1824, it had just 38 paintings on display.
- **Contact:**
- **Tel:** 020 7747 2885
- **Web:** www.nationalgallery.org.uk
- **Instagram:** @nationalgallery

Tate Britain

- **What is it?** Known as The National Gallery of British Art from 1897 to 1932, the Tate Britain as we know it now is the world center for understanding and enjoying British art.
- **Where is it?** Millbank, London SW1P 4RG
- **When to visit?** Late on Fridays
- **Nearest tube station:** Pimlico
- **Interesting fact:** The site where Tate Britain stands was a prison between 1816 and 1842.
- **Contact:**
- **Tel:** 020 7887 8888
- **Web:** www.tate.org.uk
- **Instagram:** @tatebritainlondon

Wallace Collection

- **What is it?** It is one of the smaller galleries in the city that gives a glamorous glimpse of 18th-century aristocratic life.
- **Where is it?** Hertford House, Manchester Square, London W1U 3BN
- **When to visit?** Early weekday mornings
- **Nearest tube station:** Bond Street
- **Interesting fact:** It is home to some of the most incredible Renaissance arms and armor on display.
- **Contact:**
- **Tel:** 020 7563 9500
- **Web:** www.wallacecollection.org
- **Instagram:** @wallacemuseum

Wellcome Collection

- **What is it?** It is a museum and library, founded in 2007, that displays artwork exploring the connection between art, life, and medicine, as well as medical artifacts.
- **Where is it?** 183 Euston Road, University of London, London NW1 2BE
- **When to visit?** The gallery is closed on Mondays, so any other weekday morning at opening time.
- **Nearest tube station:** Euston Square

- **Interesting fact:** The museum is named after Henry Wellcome, an American arriviste, who was knighted in Britain after establishing a pharmaceutical company and established the Wellcome trust in his will to fund health research.
- **Contact:**
- **Tel:** 020 7611 2222
- **Web:** wellcomecollection.org
- **Instagram:** @wellcomecollection

Whitechapel Gallery

- **What is it?** It is a gallery full of great ideas and art from around the world, housed in a beautifully historic building.
- **Where is it?** 77-82 Whitechapel High Street, London E1 7QX
- **When to visit?** Late Thursday nights
- **Nearest tube station:** Aldgate East
- **Interesting fact:** The Whitechapel was one of the first galleries in London to be awarded public funding to display temporary exhibitions.
- **Contact:**
- **Tel:** 020 7522 7888
- **Web:** www.whitechapelgallery.org
- **Instagram:** @whitechapelgallery

Guildhall Art Gallery and Roman Amphitheatre

- **What is it?** It is a stone, semi-Gothic Museum that houses the City of London's art collection.
- **Where is it?** Guildhall Yard, London EC2V 5AE
- **When to visit?** Early weekday mornings
- **Nearest tube station:** Bank
- **Interesting fact:** Archeologists found the Roman amphitheater in 1988 after over 100 years of searching.
- **Contact:**
- **Tel:** 020 7332 3700
- **Web:** www.cityoflondon.gov.uk
- **Instagram:** @guildhallartlondon

Serpentine Gallery

- **What is it?** It is an art gallery that hosts temporary exhibits from around the world on either side of Serpentine Lake.
- **Where is it?** Kensington Gardens
- **When to visit?** Early morning on weekdays
- **Nearest tube station:** Paddington
- **Interesting fact:** Every summer, a different architect creates a new pavilion to function as a cafe and venue for live events.
- **Contact:**
- **Tel:** 020 7402 6075
- **Web:** serpentinegalleries.org

- **Instagram:** @serpentineuk

Photographers Gallery

- **What is it?** It is the first public gallery in the UK devoted purely to photography.
- **Where is it?** 16-18 Ramillies St, London W1F 7LW
- **When to visit?** Weekday mornings
- **Nearest tube station:** Oxford Circus
- **Interesting fact:** Sue Davies, OBE, founded the gallery back in 1971.
- **Contact:**
- **Tel:** 020 7087 9300
- **Web:** thephotographersgallery.org.uk
- **Instagram:** @thephotographersgallery

Parks and Gardens

Hyde Park

- **What is it?** It is a Grade-I listed park that spans more than 350 acres.
- **Where is it?** Westminster
- **When to visit?** During either summer (but it will be really busy) or autumn when it will be slightly less so
- **Nearest tube station:** Hyde Park Corner

- **Interesting fact:** It was a hunting ground for Henry VIII before being turned into a public park by King Charles I in 1637.
- **Contact:**
- **Tel:** 0300 061 2000
- **Web:** https://www.royalparks.org.uk/visit/parks/hyde-park#about
- **Instagram:** @hydeparkldn

Richmond Park

- **What is it?** It is the biggest of London's Royal Parks, having been founded by Charles I as a deer park in the 17th century.
- **Where is it?** Richmond
- **When to visit?** Autumn for the morning mist
- **Nearest tube station:** Kew Gardens
- **Interesting fact:** Although it is no longer specifically a deer park, deer are still rife in the park.
- **Contact:**
- **Tel:** 0300 061 2200
- **Web:** https://www.royalparks.org.uk/visit/parks/richmond-park#about
- **Instagram:** @richmond_parky

Greenwich Park

- **What is it?** It is a former hunting park that covers 183 acres.
- **Where is it?** Greenwich
- **When to visit?** Fridays so you can make the most of the markets on offer
- **Nearest tube station:** Greenwich Park
- **Interesting fact:** Greenwich Park is very sporty, with the likes of cricket, tennis, and even boating being enjoyed. No signs deterring ball games here.
- **Contact:**
- **Tel:** 0300 061 2380
- **Web:** https://www.royalparks.org.uk/visit/parks/greenwich-park#about
- **Instagram:** @greenwichpark

Holland Park

- **What is it?** It is a stunning park in the West of London.
- **Where is it?** Kensington and Chelsea
- **When to visit?** Either in the summer for performances in the park's open-air theater or the spring when the tulips are in full bloom
- **Nearest tube station:** Holland Park
- **Interesting fact:** The commerce of Kyoto gifted the Kyoto Garden to the city of London in 1991, representing the friendship between Japan and

Great Britain. The garden includes koi carp, Japanese maple trees, and a peaceful bridge.

- **Contact:**
- **Tel:** 020 7602 2226
- **Web:** https://www.rbkc.gov.uk/parks-leisure-and-culture/parks/holland-park
- **Instagram:** @holland_park

St. Dunstan in the East Garden

- **What is it?** It is a public garden that is located within the ruins of St. Dunstan in the East church that was destroyed during World War II.
- **Where is it?** City of London
- **When to visit?** Early mornings before all the Instagrammers pile in
- **Nearest tube station:** Monument Station
- **Interesting fact:** The Church was a Grade-I listed building and originally built around 1100.
- **Contact:**
- **Web:** www.cityoflondon.gov.uk

Regent's Park

- **What is it?** It is a 410-acre Royal Park of London.
- **Where is it?** Camden
- **When to visit?** Between April and October, from 10:30 a.m. to 6 p.m. to make use of the boating lake.

- **Nearest tube station:** Regent's Park
- **Interesting fact:** The "Music for Trees" app will play different music created by students of the Royal Academy of Music depending on what trees you are near to add a unique element to your time there.
- **Contact:**
- **Tel:** 0300 061 2300
- **Web:** https://www.royalparks.org.uk/visit/parks/regents-park-primrose-hill?gad=1#about
- **Instagram:** @the_regents_park

St. James's Park

- **What is it?** It is a 57-acre urban park.
- **Where is it?** St. James's Park, London SW1A 2BJ
- **When to visit?** The glorious summertime (just check the website in case of any events taking place).
- **Nearest tube station:** St. James's Park
- **Interesting fact:** Henry VIII bought the land in 1532 and transformed it into personal duck-shooting and deer-hunting grounds. James I would later introduce a camel, elephant, and crocodiles in 1603.
- **Contact:**
- **Tel:** 0300 061 2350
- **Web:** https://www.royalparks.org.uk/visit/parks/st-jamess-park#about

- **Instagram:** @stjameslondon

Hampstead Heath

- **What is it?** It is a wild park made of meadows and woodland with stunning views of the city.
- **Where is it?** Camden
- **When to visit?** The summer, if you fancy a swim, or in the fall for peak foliage
- **Nearest tube station:** Hampstead
- **Interesting fact:** C.S. Lewis was supposedly inspired by Hampstead Heath when creating Narnia.
- **Contact:**
- **Tel:** 020 7332 3322
- **Web:** https://www.cityoflondon.gov.uk/things-to-do/green-spaces/hampstead-heath
- **Instagram:** @colhampsteadheath

Kensington Gardens

- **What is it?** It is a 264-acre garden that was once the private gardens of Kensington Palace.
- **Where is it?** Kensington and Chelsea
- **When to visit?** Spring so you can enjoy the flowers in full bloom, with the late afternoon giving you your best chance of avoiding big crowds.
- **Nearest tube station:** High Street Kensington

- **Interesting fact:** The picturesque gardens have been used in a whole host of films, such as *Finding Neverland, Bridget Jones: The Edge of Reason,* and *Greystroke: The Legend of Tarzan, Lord of the Apes.*
- **Contact:**
- **Tel:** 0300 061 2000
- **Web:** https://www.royalparks.org.uk/visit/parks/kensington-gardens?gad=1#about
- **Instagram:** @kgs_garden

Battersea Park

- **What is it?** It is a 200-acre park that rests on the south bank of the Thames.
- **Where is it?** Wandsworth
- **When to visit?** Nighttime is best due to the park being well-lit and offering stunning night views of the River Thames and the nearby city.
- **Nearest tube station:** Battersea Power Station
- **Interesting fact:** The park also contains a kid's zoo.
- **Contact:**
- **Tel:** 020 8871 7530
- **Web:** www.wandsworth.gov.uk
- **Instagram:** @batterseaparklondon

Sights

Changing of the Guard

- **What is it?** It is a ceremony to mark the changing of the guard between soldiers that are on duty.
- **Where is it?** Buckingham Palace
- **When to visit?** 10:45 a.m. on Mondays, Wednesdays, Fridays, and Sundays
- **Nearest tube station:** St. James's Park
- **Interesting fact:** The marching military band that accompanies the ceremony's origins dates back to playing music to boost morale and provide a beat for soldiers to march into battle to.
- **Contact:**
- **Web:** changing-guard.com
- **Instagram:** @thechangingoftheguard

Platform 9¾

- **What is it?** It is the filming location of the infamous platform 9¾ from the Harry Potter franchise.
- **Where is it?** Kings Cross Station
- **When to visit?** Avoid visiting during school holidays and try to get there before 9 a.m.; it gets very busy.
- **Nearest tube station:** Kings Cross Station

- **Interesting fact:** After you have snapped some photos, there's a platform 9¾ shop to visit, too.
- **Contact:**
- **Instagram:** @platform9and34

Trafalgar Square

- **What is it?** It is a public square established in the early 19th century with iconic fountains.
- **Where is it?** City of Westminster
- **When to visit?** It is always busy, but late afternoon will give you the best chance for some breathing room.
- **Nearest tube station:** Charing Cross
- **Interesting fact:** The square is named after the Battle of Trafalgar, which was fought in 1805 and regarded as one of Britain's most famous military victories.
- **Contact:**
- **Tel:** 020 7983 4750
- **Instagram:** @trafalgar_square_

Abbey Road

- **What is it?** It is a famous road in North London that features the iconic Abbey Road recording studios.
- **Where is it?** Camden

- **When to visit?** Weekend mornings while all the other tourists are sleeping.
- **Nearest tube station:** St. John's Wood
- **Interesting fact:** Abbey Road also features the famous zebra crossing from the "Abbey Road" album by The Beatles.
- **Contact:** Not applicable

Little Venice

- **What is it?** It is a peaceful area on Regent's Canal, with waterside pubs, cafes, and boat trips on offer.
- **Where is it?** Westminster
- **When to visit?** Anytime, perhaps September, if you are a classical music fan for reasons that will soon become known.
- **Nearest tube station:** Warwick Avenue
- **Interesting fact:** Little Venice hosts a classical music festival every September.
- **Contact:**
- **Instagram:** @littlevenice_london

Epping Forest

- **What is it?** It is a stunning, tranquil, 8,000-acre woodland that includes walking trails, rivers, and ponds.
- **Where is it?** Epping
- **When to visit?** Between January and May

- **Nearest tube station:** Epping
- **Interesting fact:** Epping forest was declared a Royal Forest by Henry II during the 12th century.
- **Contact:**
- **Web:** www.visiteppingforest.org
- **Instagram:** @coleppingforest

Columbia Road Flower Market

- **What is it?** It is a street market on a road of Victorian shops that sells bulbs, house plants, flowers, and shrubs.
- **Where is it?** Bethnal Green
- **When to visit?** The market is open every Sunday between 8 a.m. and 3 p.m. Going early will mean fewer crowds, whereas going later might mean there are better deals to be had. It is up to you to decide between fewer people or less expenditure.
- **Nearest tube station:** Bethnal Green
- **Interesting fact:** Starting as a Saturday trading market, the growing Jewish population saw the market expand onto Sundays, too, before the Saturday offering died out. The market was initially popular due to the people not having gardens big enough to grow the flowers themselves.

- **Contact:**
- **Web:** columbiaroad.info
- **Instagram:** @columbia_road_flower_market

Barbican Conservatory

- **What is it?** It is a glass-roofed, leafy sanctuary that features birds, exotic fish, and tropical plants and trees on level three of the Barbican center.
- **Where is it?** Barbican
- **When to visit?** Anytime, provided you book a timeslot.
- **Nearest tube station:** Barbican
- **Interesting fact:** The conservatory houses around 1,500 species of trees and plants, but the first batch was planted back in 1980 and 1981 before it opened its doors for the first time in 1984.
- **Contact:**
- **Tel:** 020 7870 2500
- **Web:** www.barbican.org.uk
- **Instagram:** @barbicancentre

Public Viewing Gallery at the Oxo Tower

- **What is it?** It is a free viewing platform hidden in Waterloo's Oxo Tower.
- **Where is it?** Waterloo
- **When to visit?** Any day, at any time of the year, at sunset (you won't regret it).

- **Nearest tube station:** Southwark
- **Interesting fact:** Getting there is easy and delightfully free. Just step into the lift, ascend to the eighth floor, and ask to be shown to the viewing gallery. You can even grab a bite to eat after at the restaurant that's on the same floor.
- **Contact:** Not applicable

Sky Garden

- **What is it?** It is London's highest public garden with unmatched and unmissable views of the city.
- **Where is it?** At the very top of the Fenchurch building
- **When to visit?** Same as above, any day or time of year, but try to catch the sunset here. Instantly Instagrammable and completely unforgettable.
- **Nearest tube station:** Monument
- **Interesting fact:** The building was, in fact, supposed to be even taller until concern grew about the added height affecting the view of St. Paul's Cathedral.
- **Contact:**
- **Tel:** 0333 772 0020
- **Web:** skygarden.london
- **Instagram:** @sg_skygarden

PAID

Historic

Westminster Abbey

- **What is it?** It is an iconic Anglican church.
- **How much is it? $**35
- **Where is it?** Dean's Yard, London SW1P 3PA
- **When to visit?** Around 2:30 p.m., as the crowds start to dissipate.
- **Nearest tube station:** Westminster Station
- **Interesting fact:** Westminster Abbey was originally formed during the middle of the 10th century by Benedictine monks, and their tradition of daily worship is still upheld today.
- **Contact:**
- **Tel:** 020 7222 5152
- **Web:** www.westminster-abbey.org
- **Instagram:** @westminsterabbeylondon

Tower of London

The Tower of London

- **What is it?** It is an iconic castle and World Heritage site that was originally built all the way back in 1097.
- **How much is it? $**43
- **Where is it?** Tower of London, London, EC3N 4AB
- **When to visit?** Early in the mornings to avoid lines.
- **Nearest tube station:** Tower Hill
- **Interesting fact:** The crown jewels have been locked up there since the 1600s.

- **Contact:**
- **Tel:** 0333 320 6000
- **Web:** https://www.hrp.org.uk/tower-of-london/#gs.4hd3on
- **Instagram:** @thetoweroflondon

Buckingham Palace

- **What is it?** It is the administrative headquarters of the British Monarchy.
- **How much is it?** $39–$43
- **Where is it?** Buckingham Palace, London SW1A 1AA
- **When to visit?** Summer is known as the primary touring time, meaning the State Rooms will be accessible during your trip.
- **Nearest tube station:** St. James's Park
- **Interesting fact:** Esteemed architect John Nash went way over budget when designing the palace, so far over budget in fact, that he was removed from the project.
- **Contact:**
- **Tel:** 0303 123 7300
- **Web:** www.rct.uk
- **Instagram:** @buckinghampalace.official

Kensington Palace

- **What is it?** It is a Royal residence that functions as both the London residence and offices of the Duke and Duchess of Cambridge.
- **How much is it?** $33
- **Where is it?** Kensington Gardens, London W8 4PX
- **When to visit?** Around 2 p.m. after lunch to allow big touring groups to pass through.
- **Nearest tube station:** Queensway
- **Interesting fact:** Queen Victoria was born there, and the palace contains exhibitions and displays so that visitors can explore her early life.
- **Contact:**
- **Tel:** 0333 320 6000
- **Web:** https://www.hrp.org.uk/kensington-palace/#gs.4hd4ma

Hampton Court Palace

- **What is it?** It is a Grade-I listed Royal Palace that was inhabited by Henry VIII in the 1530s.
- **How much is it?** $34–$39
- **Where is it?** Hampton Ct Way, Molesey, East Molesey KT8 9AU
- **When to visit?** Between winter and early spring, when it is usually quieter.

- **Nearest tube station:** There is no tube station to travel directly to Hampton Court, but there are trains that depart from Waterloo station that will take you to Hampton train station.
- **Interesting fact:** The palace was originally designed by Thomas Wolsey, Henry VIII's closest advisor, for himself. Once rumors started flying that it was much nicer than any of Henry's palaces, Wolsey pretended it was meant for Henry the entire time and probably avoided a beheading in the process.
- **Contact:**
- **Tel:** 020 3166 6000
- **Web:** https://www.hrp.org.uk/hampton-court-palace/#gs.4hd4sf
- **Instagram:** @hamptoncourtpalace

The Houses of Parliament

- **What is it?** It is the meeting place for the House of Commons and the House of Lords, the two houses of Parliament in the UK.
- **How much is it?** $29
- **Where is it?** London SW1A 0AA
- **When to visit?** Anytime
- **Nearest tube station:** Westminster
- **Interesting fact:** The floors of many of the rooms have old markings that are roughly two swords' lengths apart to help deter fighting.

- **Contact:**
- **Tel:** 020 7219 3000
- **Web:** www.parliament.uk
- **Instagram:** @ukparliament

St. Paul's Cathedral

- **What is it?** It is an Anglican cathedral that's Grade-I listed and serves as the Diocese of London's mother church.
- **How much is it?** $26–$30
- **Where is it?** St. Paul's Churchyard, London EC4M 8AD
- **When to visit?** Weekdays before noon
- **Nearest tube station:** St. Paul's
- **Interesting fact:** The design of the dome means that sound carries so well across the "whispering gallery" that you can whisper from one side to another.
- **Contact:**
- **Tel:** 020 7246 8350
- **Web:** www.stpauls.co.uk
- **Instagram:** @stpaulscathedrallondon

Tower Bridge

- **What is it?** It is a Grade-I listed suspension bridge and bascule that was originally constructed between 1886 and 1894.

- **How much is it? $**16
- **Where is it?** Tower Bridge Rd, London SE1 2UP
- **When to visit?** Early weekend mornings or late afternoon to evening during the week.
- **Nearest tube station:** Tower Hill
- **Interesting fact:** The bridge's construction took eight years and cost over one million pounds.
- **Contact:**
- **Tel:** 020 7403 3761
- **Web:** www.towerbridge.org.uk
- **Instagram:** @towerbridge

Churchill War Rooms

- **What is it?** It is a museum made up of the "cabinet war rooms" that was a British command center during World War II and a "Churchill Museum" that explores his life.
- **How much is it? $**35
- **Where is it?** King Charles St, London SW1A 2AQ
- **When to visit?** Between November and March
- **Nearest tube station:** Westminster
- **Interesting fact:** Churchill's war cabinet met there 115 times between the 27th of August 1939 and the 16th of August 1945.
- **Contact:**
- **Tel:** 020 7416 5000
- **Web:** www.iwm.org.uk
- **Instagram:** @imperialwarmuseums

Shakespeare's Globe

- **What is it?** It is a reconstruction of the Elizabethan playhouse that William Shakespeare wrote his plays for.
- **How much is it? $32**
- **Where is it?** 21 New Globe Walk, London SE1 9DT
- **When to visit?** Most shows take place between the months of April and October, as the theater is open-air.
- **Nearest tube station:** London Bridge
- **Interesting fact:** Shakespeare's Globe was built just yards from the site of The Globe Theatre that it is paying homage to.
- **Contact:**
- **Tel:** 020 7401 9919
- **Web:** www.shakespearesglobe.com
- **Instagram:** @the_globe

Modern

Warner Bros. Studio Tour London: The Making of Harry Potter

- **What is it?** Harry Potter fans rejoice! From the set of Diagon Alley to early concept drawings of the characters, it is all here and part of the journey into the making of Harry Potter.

- **How much is it?** $66
- **Where is it?** Studio Tour Dr, Leavesden, Watford WD25 7LR
- **When to visit?** Weekdays outside of school hours
- **Nearest tube station:** Watford Junction
- **Interesting fact:** They serve the butterbeer that Hagrid adores—although I wouldn't recommend drinking it!
- **Contact:**
- **Tel:** 0800 640 4550
- **Web:** www.wbstudiotour.co.uk
- **Instagram:** @wbtourlondon

Shrek's Adventure! London

- **What is it?** It is an immersive and interactive Shrek experience with live shows and 3D and 4D elements.
- **How much is it?** $38–$42
- **Where is it?** Riverside Building, County Hall, Westminster Bridge Rd, London SE1 7PB
- **When to visit?** First or last admissions are usually quieter.
- **Nearest tube station:** Westminster
- **Interesting fact:** If you are planning on enjoying lots of different attractions, you can group Shrek's Adventure with others, such as the SEA LIFE center, for a discount.

- **Contact:**
- **Web:** www.shreksadventure.com
- **Instagram:** @shreksadventure

Madame Tussauds London

- **What is it?** It is an incredible collection of famous faces immortalized in wax. They are ridiculously realistic, meaning there'll be lots of opportunities for photos, and you soon won't forget your experience there.
- **How much is it? $**46
- **Where is it?** Marylebone Rd, London NW1 5LR
- **When to visit?** Either early weekday mornings or late afternoons.
- **Nearest tube station:** Baker Street
- **Interesting fact:** Every wax statue takes six months and is developed using over 300 individual photographs to capture the subject's height, weight, and other intricacies like blemishes and scars.
- **Contact:**
- **Web:** www.madametussauds.com
- **Instagram:** @madametussauds

SEA LIFE London

- **What is it?** It is an aquarium with a whole host of sea creatures on display, touching stations where you can get even closer to some of them, and exhibits on sharks, penguins, and much more.

- **How much is it?** $38
- **Where is it?** Riverside Building, County Hall, Westminster Bridge Rd, London SE1 7PB
- **When to visit?** Outside of school holidays, preferably mid-week.
- **Nearest tube station:** Westminster
- **Interesting fact:** The aquarium is home to over 500 different species.
- **Contact:**
- **Tel:** 020 7967 8025
- **Web:** www.visitsealife.com
- **Instagram:** @sea_life_london

London Zoo

- **What is it?** It is a zoo, but not just any zoo. Located inside Hyde Park, it is the perfect spot for a picnic before exploring the deceptively big zoo and learning about its furry residents.
- **How much is it?** $40
- **Where is it?** Outer Cir, London NW1 4RY
- **When to visit?** Weekdays—the earlier, the better.
- **Nearest tube station:** Camden Town
- **Interesting fact:** London Zoo is the oldest scientific zoo in the world.
- **Contact:**
- **Tel:** 0344 225 1826

- **Web:** www.londonzoo.org
- **Instagram:** @zsllondonzoo

The London Dungeon

- **What is it?** It is a historical tourist attraction that recreates gory historical events in a humorous style using rides, special effects, and even live actors. It is as fun as it is educational.
- **How much is it?** $43
- **Where is it?** Riverside Building, County Hall, Westminster Bridge Rd, London SE1 7PB
- **When to visit?** The first and last admissions should be quieter.
- **Nearest tube station:** Waterloo Station
- **Interesting fact:** The attraction features over 1,000 years of London's gruesome history.
- **Contact:**
- **Tel:** 020 7967 8022
- **Web:** https://www.thedungeons.com/london/
- **Instagram:** @londondungeon

Wembley Stadium Tour

- **What is it?** It is England's national stadium and the home of the national soccer team. Taking in a game would be quite an experience, but their stadium tours are special, too, and are on offer all year round.

- **How much is it?** $31
- **Where is it?** London HA9 0WS
- **When to visit?** Anytime
- **Nearest tube station:** Wembley Park
- **Interesting fact:** Wembley stadium has 90,000 seats, making it the biggest sports venue in the UK and the second biggest in all of Europe.
- **Contact:**
- **Tel:** 0800 169 9933
- **Web:** www.wembleystadium.com
- **Instagram:** @wembleystadium

Queen Elizabeth Olympic Park Stadium Tour

- **What is it?** It is a purpose-built sporting complex and public park that hosted the Olympic games in 2012.
- **How much is it?** $25
- **Where is it?** London E20 2ST
- **When to visit?** Weekdays in the morning
- **Nearest tube station:** Stratford
- **Interesting fact:** The stadium now operates primarily as the home of Premier League soccer team West Ham United, but the oval shape and retractable seats means that it can be reconfigured for a whole host of events such as concerts, baseball, or cricket.
- **Contact:**
- **Tel:** 020 8522 6000

- **Web:** www.london-stadium.com
- **Instagram:** @londonstadium

ArcelorMittal Orbit

- **What is it?** It is a sculpture and observation tower that functions as a slide and abseiling attraction.
- **How much is it?** $25 for sliding and $83 for abseiling
- **Where is it?** Queen Elizabeth Olympic Park, 5 Thornton St, London E20 2AD
- **When to visit?** Anytime, just be sure to book first.
- **Nearest tube station:** Stratford
- **Interesting fact:** It is over 114 meters tall.
- **Contact:**
- **Tel:** 0333 800 8099
- **Web:** arcelormittalorbit.com/
- **Instagram:** @amorbit

National Theater

- **What is it?** It is one of the three most prominently funded performing arts venues in the UK.
- **How much is it?** Admission is free, but the prices for various shows and events vary.
- **Where is it?** London SE1 9PX
- **When to visit?** Anytime
- **Nearest tube station:** Waterloo

- **Interesting fact:** The National Theater was opened to the public in 1976.
- **Contact:**
- **Tel:** 020 3989 5455
- **Web:** www.nationaltheatre.org.uk/
- **Instagram:** @nationaltheatre

Experiences

The London Eye

- **What is it?** It is the tallest cantilevered observation wheel in Europe that provides unrivaled views of its most beautiful city (although I am a little biased).
- **How much is it? $**52
- **Where is it?** Riverside Building, County Hall, London SE1 7PB
- **When to visit?** Early morning or late evening are less busy, with London looking particularly magical at night.
- **Nearest tube station:** Waterloo
- **Interesting fact:** With over three million paid visitors every single year, the London Eye is the most popular paid visitor attraction in the UK.
- **Contact:**
- **Tel:** 020 7967 8021
- **Web:** www.londoneye.com
- **Instagram:** @londoneye

IFS Cloud Cable Car

- **What is it?** It is the only urban cable car in the UK.
- **How much is it?** $8–$15
- **Where is it?** Greenwich Peninsula
- **When to visit?** The peninsula is beautiful at night.
- **Nearest tube station:** North Greenwich
- **Interesting fact:** Since opening in 2012, cable cars have welcomed tens of millions of passengers.
- **Contact:**
- **Tel:** 0343 222 1234
- **Web:** https://tfl.gov.uk/modes/london-cable-car/

The View From The Shard

- **What is it?** It is exactly what it says on the tin! There's an observation deck between the 68th and 72nd floor on The Shard, and the views are wonderful.
- **How much is it?** $36
- **Where is it?** 32 London Bridge St, London SE1 9SG
- **When to visit?** Either at sunset or at night, take your pick.
- **Nearest tube station:** London Bridge
- **Interesting fact:** The View from The Shard spans three floors: the 68th, 69th, and 72nd. There's an indoor viewing gallery, interactive multimedia

"tell:scopes" (interactive telescopes), and an open-air Skydeck on the 72nd floor.

- **Contact:**
- **Tel:** 0344 499 7222
- **Web:** www.theviewfromtheshard.com
- **Instagram:** @shardview

Up at The O2

- **What is it?** It is a guided climb across the roof of the O2 with stunning scenic views of city landmarks.
- **How much is it? $**45
- **Where is it?** Peninsula Square, London SE10 0DX
- **When to visit?** Going on the weekdays will prevent you from feeling rushed by large groups.
- **Nearest tube station:** North Greenwich
- **Interesting fact:** The climb is an immersive 90-minute experience, making it well worth the money.
- **Contact:**
- **Tel:** 020 8463 2680
- **Web:** www.theo2.co.uk
- **Instagram:** @upattheo2

The London Bridge Experience and London Tombs

- **What is it?** It is an actor-led tourist attraction that takes visitors on a tour through London's rich history, including Boudicca's battles with the Romans and The Great Fire of London.

- **How much is it? $38**
- **Where is it?** The Rennie Vaults, 2-4 Tooley St, London SE1 2SY
- **When to visit?** Weekdays after 3 p.m. Between July and August are the attraction's peak season, so try to avoid visiting between those months if possible.
- **Nearest tube station:** London Bridge
- **Interesting fact:** The London Tombs can be scary, with actors jumping out at you at every turn; however, for those who want to enjoy the blood and gore a little more peacefully, there's also the "Guardian Angel Tour" that doesn't include actors chasing you around.
- **Contact:**
- **Tel:** 020 7403 6333
- **Web:** thelondonbridgeexperience.com
- **Instagram:** @thelondonbridgeexperience

SIGHTSEEING TOURS

You can find additional information on all of the following tours, including booking information, at https://www.viator.com/London-tours/City-Tours/d737-g12-c5330

Big Bus London Hop-On Hop-Off Tour and River Cruise

- **What is it?** It is an open-top double-decker bus tour that includes Hyde Park, St. Paul's Cathedral, and Buckingham Palace.
- **How long is it?** Between 1 hour and 10 minutes and 3 hours and 30 minutes.
- **How much is it?** From $52

Westminster to Greenwich Sightseeing Thames Cruise in London

- **What is it?** It is a Thames sightseeing cruise that starts in Westminster and ends in Greenwich.
- **How long is it?** 1 hour
- **How much is it?** $20

Best of London Including Tower of London and Changing of the Guard

- **What is it?** It is an extensive London tour that includes a visit to the Tower of London, a tour of St. Paul's Cathedral, a photo opportunity at Westminster Abbey, and a chance to experience the Changing of the Guard at Buckingham Palace.
- **How long is it?** A maximum of 9 hours depending on add-ons and extras
- **How much is it?** From $159

Original Harry Potter Locations Tour

- **What is it?** It is a tour of filming locations from the Harry Potter franchise that includes movie trivia and a fun quiz at the end to test your listening skills.
- **How long is it?** 2 hours
- **How much is it?** $26

Jack the Ripper Tour With "Ripper Vision"

- **What is it?** It is a tour through Jack the Ripper's reign of terror using "ripper vision," handheld projectors that transport you right back to Victorian times.
- **How long is it?** 1 hour and 45 minutes
- **How much is it?** $23

Premier Classic London Private Half-Day Tour

- **What is it?** It is a private tour around London in a black cab—there's no need for me to list the sights you will see throughout because you will see everything.
- **How long is it?** 4 hours
- **How much is it?** From $450

Historical London Walking Tour in Westminster and Churchill War Rooms Entry

- **What is it?** It is a walking tour that immerses you in the history of World War II throughout Westminster and finishes down in the Churchill War Rooms.
- **How long is it?** 2 hours and 30 minutes
- **How much is it?** $81

London Public Busses Audio Tour

- **What is it?** It is an audio tour that's enjoyed along some of London's iconic bus routes; it is cheap, cheerful, and informative.
- **How long is it?** As long as you want it to be.
- **How much is it?** Just $8.50, making it well worth experiencing.

Changing of the Guard Walking Tour Experience

Two "Beefeaters" standing guard outside Buckingham Palace

- **What is it?** It is a walking tour that's based around the Changing of the Guard, allowing attendees to enjoy the ceremony from special vantage points while enjoying audio commentary.
- **How long is it?** 1 hour and 30 minutes

- **How much is it?** $20

London Rock Music Tour

- **What is it?** It is a tour through London's legendary rock music history that includes the houses of Ringo and Jimmy Page, Tin Pan Alley, and Abbey Road.
- **How long is it?** A maximum of 8 hours, depending on your choice of morning, afternoon, or full-day tour.
- **How much is it?** From $87

So, there's your days sorted and, quite frankly, jam-packed with things to see and do.

Bonus tip: The publication *Time Out* is everywhere in London: train seats, bookstands, and you might even find a couple riding the escalators. Grab one! They are packed full of activities, events, and interesting information that will supplement this guide. They are also available online at https://www.timeout.com/.

But what about those who are more interested in the nightlife? Or those who somehow still have the energy to drink and dance the night away after pounding the pavement all day?

Unsurprisingly, London is just as exciting at night as it is in the day.

6

NIGHTLIFE

Whether you want to dance until your feet fall off or sink into a pint by an open fire, rock out with your hair down or sip martinis to jazz as smooth as your drink or spend your night roaming from venue to venue on what the Brits call a "pub crawl," London has you covered here too.

Before we explore specific venues, let's start with some facts, none of which are more prevalent than the fact that the British love a drink…

- …which goes a long way to explaining why there are over 7,000 pubs in the City of London and the City of Westminster alone.
- "Pop Goes the Weasel" wasn't always just a harmless nursery rhyme; the original version of

the song was about someone having to pawn their suit after spending all of their money in the pub.

- Some pubs have some very famous owners; for instance, the limestone pub, The Grapes, is owned by Sir Ian McKellen.
- Five of the London Underground's tube stations were even named after pubs: Angel, Royal Oak, Manor House, Swiss Cottage, and Elephant Castle.
- Some pubs in Smithfield and Borough are licensed to serve alcohol as early as 7 a.m. due to hours worked by market porters.
- The largest owner of "boozers" in London is a Japanese bank.
- London is home to the smallest pub in the world, The Dove, which is in Hammersmith for those who fancy rubbing elbows while sipping a pint.

Remember to check the opening times of all the following locations, as they might change throughout the year and around the holidays.

Right, let's get planning that big, or small, night out, shall we?

BEST CLUBS

I think it is important to recognize that the "best" club for some will be an absolute nightmare for others; therefore, we've split each section up depending on the kind of night you are looking for. In this case, we've divided clubs up depending on the vibe you are looking for.

Raves

If you are looking for an intense rave with laser shows and thumping music, you should consider a night out at

Egg London

- **What is it?** It is a 1,000-capacity club that spans four rooms and hosts some of the biggest and best line-ups in house music. It has outdoor spaces and a 24-hour license, meaning you can quite literally dance the night away under the stars.
- **Where is it?** 5-13 Vale Royal, London, N7 9AP

Ministry of Sound

- **What is it?** It is one of London's most popular clubs, hosting some of the world's biggest DJs, spanning four rooms and with a 1,600-person capacity, this one is a can't miss for house music lovers, and just like Egg, it is open all night.
- **Where is it?** 103 Gaunt St, London SE1 6DP

Studio 338

- **What is it?** It is an Ibiza-inspired club on the gorgeous Greenwich Peninsula. It has a 3,000-person capacity and three separate arenas to choose from: terrace, loft, and garden. Oh, and it has a glass ceiling, so whether it is sunny out or a beautiful starry night, you will be able to enjoy it.
- **Where is it?** 338 Boord St, London SE10 0PF

XOYO

- **What is it?** It is an intimate club with a bar and a basement in Shoreditch. Don't be fooled by the word "intimate," though; the sound system in the basement is anything but.
- **Where is it?** 32-37 Cowper St, London EC2A 4AP

Cheese (Pop)

If cheesy pop music is more your thing and you fancy singing your heart out to Abba all night, or you are more of a fan of current hits, you will probably prefer.

The Clapham Grand

- **What is it?** It is a refurbished Victorian hall that's been entertaining excited crowds since the 1900s! Now, it not only hosts club nights with all the cheese you can handle but fun events and comedy nights, too.

- **Where is it?** 21-25, St John's Hill, London SW11 1TT

Infernos

- **What is it?** It is a fun club that's had Londoners partying since 1914! Now, it has an '80s theme, including decor and tunes, and is well-known for its bright neon lights, huge dance floor, and glittering disco balls.
- **Where is it?** 146 Clapham High St, London SW4 7UH

Carwash Nightclub

- **What is it?** It is London's longest-running pop and disco club that takes place every Saturday night with three floors of '80s, '90s, disco, party, and club music. There are even flamboyant performers, partygoers in crazy costumes, a jacuzzi, and a swimming pool!
- **Where is it?** 19 Dering St, London W1S 1AH

Queen of Hoxton

- **What is it?** It is a bar and club that hosts DJs and live music across three floors, including a rooftop garden that's considered one of the best rooftops in London, which also has a barbecue. On Thursday, they host "non-stop pop night," which will ensure you are provided with more cheese than a cheeseboard.

- **Where is it?** 1 Curtain Rd, London EC2A 3JX

Club de Fromage

- **What is it?** The name promises cheese, and cheese is what you get—a night packed with singing, confetti, dancing, and more confetti! This place considers itself the UK's "premier pop party," and once you have been, you will find it hard to argue.
- **Where is it?** 16 Parkfield St, London N1 0PZ

BEST PUBS

A typical selection of draught beers on offer in a London pub

Britain, and more specifically London, is known for its pubs (7,000 of them, as we mentioned earlier), so let's look a little closer at some that we recommend you grab a pint in.

The Angelsea Arms

- **What is it?** It is a cozy public house that's tucked away just off Ravenscourt Park. With a roaring fire, a traditional British menu, a wood-paneled bar, and five rotating real-ale pumps, it is a little slice of Great Britain away from the hubbub of the city.

- **Where is it?** 15 Selwood Terrace, South Kensington, London SW7 3QG

The Churchill Arms

- **What is it?** Decked with flowers and full of Winston Churchill memorabilia, the Churchill Arms is educational and cozy (especially at Christmas time when it is all decked out with twinkling trees and lights) and serves belly-warming Thai food.
- **Where is it?** 119 Kensington Church St, London W8 7LN

The Dove

- **What is it?** It is a pub on Broadway Market in Hackney that offers beers from all around the world, distinctly British food, and a wide selection of board games to huddle up around and leave the busyness of London.
- **Where is it?** 24-28 Broadway Market, London E8 4QJ

The French House

- **What is it?** It is a snug, Bohemian watering hole popular with artists who prefer wine to beer and adhere to a strict no-technology rule (which we could all do with from time to time, let's be honest).

- **Where is it?** 49 Dean St, London W1D 5BG

The Plough

- **What is it?** It is a refurbished Victorian pub with an 18th-century interior, roaring open fires, and British ales on tap. It is snug, away from the rat race, and serves all the British classics you'd expect.
- **Where is it?** 27 Museum St, London WC1A 1JT

Skehans Free House

- **What is it?** It is a neighborhood pub that's popular with art students and locals. Expect traditional Irish music nights, a fiercely competitive quiz night, an ever more fiercely competitive pool table, and, for those who are hungry, some great Thai food.
- **Where is it?** 1 Kitto Rd, London SE14 5SN

The Coach and Horses

- **What is it?** It is a Soho pub with a regularly played piano and threadbare decor that's charmingly stuck in the past. If you fancy a sing-along around

a piano with a pint in one hand and a pickled egg in the other, this is your pub.
- **Where is it?** 29 Greek St, London W1D 5DH

The Cow

- **What is it?** It is an unpretentious gastropub in Notting Hill with upstairs dining that has a minimal menu consisting mainly of seafood scribbled on a chalkboard and doesn't take reservations. The downstairs pub is as straightforward as the menu, with small tables surrounded by stools of punters drinking British and Belgian beer.
- **Where is it?** 89 Westbourne Park Rd, London W2 5QH

The Duke

- **What is it?** It is a pub tucked away from the museumgoers in Bloomsbury. It is styled with '30s decor and painted in eye-watering rhubarb. A detour from the hipster-filled pubs serving foams and shards, this place serves pie and mash as a staple, and its locals can be found curled up with a newspaper. It is quiet, offering a welcome reprieve from the other tourists you will be fighting for photo opportunities with.
- **Where is it?** 7 Roger St, London WC1N 2PB

Our last pub is much, much more than just a pub.

The Ivy House

- **What is it?** It is a pub with a story as heartwarming as the open fire inside it. The Ivy House became the first cooperatively owned pub in London when its community helped the tenants raise a million pounds to prevent it from being sold off to developers. Today, it is an establishment that offers ale brewed locally and holds community events from raucous live music to knitting clubs. A feel-good story and a feel-good pub.
- **Where is it?** 40 Stuart Rd, London SE15 3BE

BEST BARS

London is awash with all kinds of bars! Rather than leaving you struggling to know where to turn, we've divided this list into subcategories so we can recommend the best bars for each niche.

Karaoke

We all love a bit of karaoke, don't we? Well, we here at World of Wunder Travel do anyway! If, like us, you love doing your best Madonna impression on a Saturday night, these bars are for you.

The Star Liverpool Street

- **What is it?** It is a karaoke bar with locations in both Liverpool Street and Bethnal Green. There's beer, wine, and cocktails. Smoked meat for those that are peckish. Most importantly, when it comes to the karaoke itself, there are more than 20,000 songs to choose from and five uniquely decorated rooms to sing in.
- **Where is it?** 94 Middlesex St, London E1 7EZ

Karaoke Box Smithfield

- **What is it?** It is a karaoke bar with touch screens and wireless microphones, 14 private rooms to choose from, a cocktail bar, and songs in English, Japanese, and Arabic. There are also Karaoke Box locations in Mayfair and Soho if you aren't staying near Smithfield.
- **Where is it?** 12 Smithfield St, London EC1A 9LA

The Old Queens Head

- **What is it?** It is a great option for those who can't deal with all these swanky new karaoke bars and just want to crowd into the back room of a pub and sing their hearts out to a great selection of songs (with a host, of course).
- **Where is it?** 44 Essex Rd, London N1 8LN

Rock Music

Want somewhere loud that you can't hear your friends talk or yourself think? Look no further!

The Electric Ballroom

- **What is it?** It is an energetic and raucous live music venue in the heart of Camden. With an upstairs bar, club nights, and live performances that have featured legendary acts such as Blink 182 and Sid Vicious in the past, this place rocks, and the daytime market that it hosts on weekends is well worth checking out too.
- **Where is it?** 184 Camden High St, London NW1 8QP

The Underworld

- **What is it?** Sticking in Camden, The Underworld is a gritty basement club that offers cheap booze, rock 'n' roll music, and a dance floor for live music in the very depths of the venue.
- **Where is it?** 174 Camden High St, London NW1 9DL

The Fighting Cocks

- **What is it?** A rock bar with live music and an even livelier crowd. With a cracking selection on the

jukebox, free *Guitar Hero* on offer, and a leopard-print pool table, the place is absolutely buzzing with personality and should be the first pub in the itinerary for the rockers amongst you.
- **Where is it?** 56 Old London Rd, Kingston upon Thames KT2 6QA

Cocktails

Here are some options for those of you who value majestically mixed cocktails above all else.

The Alchemist

- **What is it?** With multiple venues across London, the Alchemist is a restaurant and bar that combines science with the art of cocktail making and is an incredibly unique experience. From Bunsen burners and blowtorches to being served drinks in flasks and jam jars. Every element of the cocktail-making process takes place right in front of you and is well worth a picture or two for your socials.
- **Where is it?** 145 City Rd, London EC1V 1LP

Bar Américain Soho

- **What is it?** It is a more conventional and intimate cocktail bar for those who don't want sparklers hanging out of or a blowtorch taken to their

drinks. This place is elegant, with art deco fittings that have hardly changed in decades. Its lounge setting is very cozy, too, with luxurious leather sofas.
- **Where is it?** 20 Sherwood St, London W1F 7ED

The Connaught Bar

- **What is it?** Fancy is what it is, real fancy. The Connaught is a swanky hotel bar with huge mirrors and Cubist-inspired wood paneling, the type of place where martinis are made right in front of you. Great for those traveling with a somewhat unlimited budget.
- **Where is it?** 16 Carlos Pl, London W1K 2AL

Sports

The British love their sports; therefore, the number of sports bars across the capital is no surprise. Sports bars are fun, rowdy, and often surprisingly emotional places (you have been warned!).

We recommend catching a game at the following places.

Beechwood Sports Pub and Kitchen

- **What is it?** It is a lively sports pub that utilizes huge TV screens and surround sound to bring the very best of boxing, football, cricket, tennis, basketball, and just about any other sport you can think of, to their customers. There's even an outside terrace.

- **Where is it?** 1A Principal Place, Worship St, London EC2A 2FA

The Moretown Belle

- **What is it?** It is a sports bar located just minutes from the Tower of London that shows a wide range of sports across a whopping 31 screens! If watching isn't enough, there's plenty to play too, with a pool table and dart board.
- **Where is it?** 5 Thomas More St, London E1W 1YY

Boom Battle Bar

- **What is it?** It is a hybrid of a sports bar and a "battle bar." There are Boom Battle Bars across the city, and they all promise the same thing: fun! With live sports shown, the secret sauce here is the games. Pool, shuffleboard, interactive darts, and even ax-throwing are on offer, including loads more.
- **Where is it?** 70-88 Oxford Street, London, W1D 1BS

Phew! There's your lot. Whatever you decide to do, I assure you, you will end up having a great night!

Just don't forget to check opening and closing times ahead of time to avoid disappointment.

Next, we will look at the best areas to stay, as well as events, festivals, nights out, and the culture that London offers the LGBTQIA+ community.

7

LGBTQIA+

London isn't just diverse when it comes to race or religion; it is also considered the "queer capital" of the United Kingdom. This next chapter will cover everything that a member of the LGBTQIA+ community would want to know before traveling.

LANGUAGE

Let's start with the language. London pre-1970s had a secret language known as Polari to communicate since back then homosexuality was illegal. Polari was a mixture of Italian, Romani, and good old cockney rhyming slang, including words like "camp," "butch," and "queen."

Polari allowed people to be themselves safely back when the world was a much less accepting place, but that doesn't mean you won't still hear a little of it now. It is prevalent within drag culture and the many gay cabarets that are on offer throughout the city and stand as a testament to London's gay legacy.

BEST AREAS TO STAY IN

London is a very accepting place; however, that doesn't mean that some places won't offer more to the LGBTQIA+ community than others. The following are the best areas of London to stay in (or visit) if you are part of it.

Soho

It is central, surrounded by cocktail bars and famous landmarks, and is gay London's premier neighborhood. Recommended hotels include:

The Z Hotel

- **Where is it?** 17 Moor St, London W1D 5AP
- **Rate range:** $150–$180
- **Interesting fact:** There are also Z hotels across the city, so they are well worth considering wherever you decide to stay.
- **Unique features:** Soundproof rooms, free Wi-Fi, and a bar and lounge
- **Nearby attractions:** Palace Theater, Pineapple Dance Studios, and The Phoenix Garden

Hazlitt's Hotel

- **Where is it?** 6 Frith St, London W1D 3JA
- **Rate range:** $359–$462
- **Interesting fact:** The gorgeous Georgian building that the hotel is housed in dates all the way back to 1718 and was named after essayist William Hazlitt.
- **Unique features:** Concierge, dry cleaning, and a minibar
- **Nearby attractions:** Soho Theater, Soho Square, and Prince Edward Theater

The Lalit Hotel

- **Where is it?** 181 Tooley St, London SE1 2JR
- **Rate range:** $205–$272
- **Interesting fact:** The Lalit is a Grade II listed building that was built more than 125 years ago by Edward Mountford, architect of the Old Bailey.
- **Unique features:** Fitness center, massage, and currency exchange
- **Nearby attractions:** Tower Bridge, Bridge Theater, and Fashion and Textile Museum

Vauxhall

Vauxhall was the original queer neighborhood of London when homosexuality was illegal, in modern day it is an area rife with LGBTQIA+ history and packed with some of the best gay bars in the city!

Where should you stay to enjoy these things? I am glad you asked!

Belgravia Hotel

- **Where is it?** 104 Ebury St, London SW1W 9QD
- **Rate range:** $125–$135
- **Interesting fact:** In an area filled with five-star hotels, this bed and breakfast represents great value in an area perfect for those in the LGBTQIA+ community.
- **Unique features:** Cooked breakfast, free Wi-Fi, and a great location
- **Nearby attractions:** Royal Court Theater, Belgrave House, and Cadogan Hall

Tophams Hotel

- **Where is it?** 24-32 Ebury St, London SW1W 0LU
- **Rate range:** $312–$444
- **Interesting fact:** This building has functioned as a hotel since the end of World War II when five Victorian houses were transformed into one.
- **Unique features:** Valet parking, wake-up service, and housekeeping
- **Nearby attractions:** Rifle Brigade Monument, Victoria Palace Theater, and Belgrave House

Comfort Inn Victoria

- **Where is it?** 18-24 A3213, Pimlico, London SW1V 1QF
- **Rate range:** $167–$193
- **Interesting fact:** Just like The Z hotel, there are Comfort Inn's across the city, so don't feel restricted to Victoria despite our recommendation.
- **Unique features:** Free Wi-Fi, air conditioning, and a breakfast buffet
- **Nearby attractions:** Westminster Cathedral, Victoria Palace Theater, and Dermoi! spa and wellness

Shoreditch

The number of LGBTQIA+ spaces in London is growing. This is no surprise, given it is a melting pot of different cultures, passions, and beliefs. Large parts of East London are the most diverse in the entire city, which is why it is well worth considering staying in Shoreditch.

Nobu Hotel

- **Where is it?** 10-50 Willow St, London EC2A 4BH
- **Rate range:** $365–$410
- **Interesting fact:** The hotel doubles as a swanky bar and terrace that mixes East London and Tokyo vibes.

- **Unique features:** Valet parking, dry cleaning, and a currency exchange
- **Nearby attractions:** Mark Street Gardens, Bunhill Fields, and Shoreditch Town Hall

Point A Shoreditch

- **Where is it?** 8-10 Paul Street, London EC2A 4JH
- **Rate range:** $132–$176
- **Interesting fact:** There are Point A hotels across the city for those who don't want to stay in Shoreditch.
- **Unique features:** Pet-friendly, air conditioning, and free Wi-Fi
- **Nearby attractions:** Exchange Square, Jealous Gallery and Print Studio, and Milton Court Concert Hall

Once you have dropped your bags off and freshened up, there are all kinds of places that will be of particular interest to the LGBTQIA+ community throughout London, from historic landmarks to modern attractions.

Culture and Museums

Gay's the Word

- **What is it?** It is the oldest LGBTQIA+ bookshop in the UK since it was established in 1979.
- **How much is it?** Free

- **Where is it?** 66 Marchmont Street, London WC1N 1AB
- **When to visit?** Anytime
- **Nearest tube station:** Euston Square
- **Interesting fact:** The shop was established in 1979 as a community space by gay socialists who funneled any profits right back into the business.
- **Contact:**
- **Tel:** 020 7278 7654
- **Web:** www.gaystheword.co.uk
- **Instagram:** @gaysthewordbookshop

Admiral Duncan Memorial

- **What is it?** It is a memorial in honor of the three people killed in the heinous 1999 nail-bomb attack on the gay pub, the Admiral Duncan.
- **How much is it?** Free
- **Where is it?** W1, Wardour Street, St Anne's Gardens
- **When to visit?** Anytime
- **Nearest tube station:** Leicester Square
- **Contact:** Not applicable

Above the Stag

- **What is it?** It is the first theater across the UK to dedicate itself to showcasing LGBTQIA theater.
- **How much is it?** $23–$28

- **Where is it?** 72 Albert Embankment, London SE1 7TP
- **When to visit?** Anytime, just book ahead.
- **Nearest tube station:** Vauxhall
- **Interesting fact:** Above the Stag Theater also produces its own shows that are all LGBT-themed.
- **Contact:**
- **Web:** abovethestag.com
- **Instagram:** @abovethestag

Queer Britain

- **What is it?** It is the UK's first LGBTQIA+ museum, dedicated to its culture, history, and future.
- **How much is it?** Free
- **Where is it?** 2 Granary Square, London N1C 4BH
- **When to visit?** Weekday mornings
- **Nearest tube station:** Kings Cross St. Pancras
- **Interesting fact:** The museum was founded in 2018 by a former editor of *Gay Times*, Joseph Galliano, and in 2019 it was registered as a charity.
- **Contact:**
- **Web:** queerbritain.org.uk
- **Instagram:** @queerbritain

Bishopsgate Institute

- **What is it?** It is a cultural institute whose archives and collections include one of the UK's most extensive looks at LGBTQIA+ culture, history, and politics from the nineteenth century onwards.
- **How much is it?** Free
- **Where is it?** 230 Bishopsgate, London EC2M 4QH
- **When to visit?** Wednesday evenings (they stay open a little later!)
- **Nearest tube station:** Liverpool Street Station
- **Interesting fact:** Bishopsgate Institute celebrated its 125th birthday in 2020.
- **Contact:**
- **Tel:** 020 7392 9200
- **Web:** www.bishopsgate.org.uk
- **Instagram:** @bishopsgateinstitute

Events and Festivals

London Pride

- **What is it?** It is the UK's biggest and most diverse festival that celebrates LGBTQ+ communities. Showcasing conferences, theater shows, exhibitions, and tours.
- **Where is it?** Haymarket
- **When is it?** July

- **How much is it?** Free

UK Black Pride

- **What is it?** It is a celebration of Asian, African, Latin American, Caribbean, and Middle Eastern heritage members of the LGBTQIA+ community.
- **Where is it?** Queen Elizabeth Olympic Park
- **When is it?** August
- **How much is it?** Free

Fringe! Queer Film and Arts Festival

- **What is it?** It is a festival that showcases and celebrates the very best of the creative arts, telling diverse LGBTQIA+ stories from all around the world.
- **Where is it?** Across East London
- **When is it?** September
- **How much is it?** Prices vary, but most of the events and screenings are completely free.

BFI: Flare

- **What is it?** It is the biggest LGBTQIA+ film festival in Europe.
- **Where is it?** BFI Southbank
- **When is it?** March

- **How much is it?** Prices vary, but a festival pass costs around $154.

Drag Fest London

- **What is it?** It is a festival celebrating drag queens that includes live music, a lip sync stage, meet and greets, shopping, and a fun fair, and that's not all.
- **Where is it?** Studio 338, Greenwich Peninsula
- **When is it?** August
- **How much is it?** From $21

Tours

A Queer History of London

- **What is it?** It is a walking tour exploring and celebrating London's queer history, including important landmarks, stories of iconic drag queens from the 1700s, the secret gay soirees from the 1920s, and the stories of the people that are still driving the desire for change and inclusivity around the world.
- **How long is it?** 2 hours
- **How much is it?** You can donate whatever you feel the tour was worth, so that's completely up to you.

LGBTQ Historical Tour Solo (Virtual)

- **What is it?** It is a virtual walking town through Soho's fabulous queer history, from the characters that have lived there to the arts, culture, science, and politics. Why not take the tour on your phone as you take the walk, too? You could even stop off at some of our recommended bars for a cocktail.
- **How long is it?** That's up to you.
- **How much is it?** Free

Thc London of Oscar Wilde

- **What is it?** It is a walking tour that explores the life and downfall of Oscar Wilde, infamous author, playwright, and member of the LGBTQIA+ community, of course.
- **How long is it?** 2 hours
- **How much is it?** $11.50

Theatreland Walking Tour

- **What is it?** It is a tour around the most iconic theaters in the West End's theatreland district that includes tales of intrigue, glamor, and stardom.
- **How long is it?** Tours are offered for both half and full days.
- **How much is it?** $256 for a half-day tour and $450 for a full day

Best Bars and Nightlife

So, now that you have an idea of where to stay and how to spend your days, let's look at some of the best LGBTQIA+ bars and clubs that London has to offer in Soho, Vauxhall, Shoreditch, and beyond.

Freedom Bar Soho

- **What is it?** It is an upscale gay bar with flowers, modern light fixtures, and comfy, plush sofas. It is classy and lavish and offers a signature cocktail menu so you can enjoy a drink as classy as your surroundings. Those of you who scoffed at the word "classy" are covered too, though; they host a drag competition show downstairs on Mondays that's much crasser and showcases some of the best drag artists in the city.
- **Where is it?** 60-66 Wardour St, London W1F 0TA

Comptons of Soho

- **What is it?** It is a place for those who prefer tacky to classy, which is to be taken as a compliment, of course. Picture rickety furniture, a creaky wooden floor, and antiquated chandeliers. It is all wonderfully outdated, and the convivial atmosphere has made it a neighborhood staple. There's also a quieter lounge upstairs for those easing their way into the night.

- **Where is it?** 51-53 Old Compton St, London W1D 6HN

She Soho

- **What is it?** It is London's only bar that's women-only and dedicated to giving lesbians a great night! There are strictly no men allowed, but the bar is trans-inclusive, and the venue is very swanky and feels futuristic, with a chilled atmosphere and DJs playing at weekends.
- **Where is it?** 23a Old Compton St, London W1D 5JL

G-A-Y Bar

- **What is it?** It is a classic, without frills and cheap drinks, with a good mix of locals and tourists. There's a friendly, welcoming vibe, pop tunes blaring until the early hours of the morning, and the added bonus of a summer terrace on the second floor.
- **Where is it?** 30 Old Compton St, London W1D 4UR

Royal Vauxhall Tavern

- **What is it?** It is an iconic cabaret hall that, according to legend, Freddie Mercury once helped sneak Princess Diana into. This place is London's oldest standing LGBTQIA+ venue, established in 1860. Today, it showcases cabaret, hosts weekly club nights, and is a great place to grab a pint.

- **Where is it?** 372 Kennington Ln, London SE11 5HY

The Cock Tavern

- **What is it?** It is a chic "Georgian tiki bar" serving delicious cocktails. A tiki bar that's housed in a Georgian pub, it is a unique blend of styles that somehow works, but I suppose most places where you can sip a cocktail in a plush leather armchair tend to.
- **Where is it?** 315 Mare St, London E8 1EJ

Dalston Superstore

- **What is it?** This place is just cool. A funky space that offers coffee and food in the daytime before morphing into an energetic bar at night that hosts live music, DJs, and a wide range of entertainment. Drag brunch is offered on the weekends, which is a must-visit, with games, quizzes, and prizes.
- **Where is it?** 117 Kingsland High St, London E8 2PB

The Queen Adelaide

- **What is it?** Quite simply, it is a strip club turned gay bar that offers some of the cheapest beer in the city at just over $5 a pint.
- **Where is it?** 483 Hackney Rd, Cambridge Heath, London E2 9ED

The Wayout Club

- **What is it?** Founded in 1993, The Wayout Club is one of London's leading transgender nightclubs with over 30 years of history, celebrated during their Saturday night events.
- **Where is it?** The White Swan, 556 Commercial Rd, London E14 7JD

That should give everybody a wide range of things to enjoy with their days, nights, and everything in between.

Remember that while you are having fun and seeing the city, it is also important to always keep yourself safe, so the next chapter will get a little more serious and cover emergencies and survival. You won't be enjoying this trip, or any trip, without staying safe!

8

EMERGENCIES AND SURVIVAL

This chapter will give you crucial information to help you with any emergencies that you might face during your trip. While London is a safe city, emergencies can still happen to anybody anywhere in the world.

Expecting the unexpected so you are prepared for anything from a lost passport to a medical emergency could be the difference between a dream trip and a living nightmare!

By the end of this chapter, you will have the know-how and peace of mind to ensure you enjoy a great trip with peace of mind.

LONDON CRIME FACTS

Before we look at tips and advice, it is important to look at some crime statistics from the first quarter of 2023

(*Crime rates*, 2023), which may influence choices on your trip or, at the very least, ensure you always keep your wits about you.

- In London's first quarter, there were a total of 894,215 crimes.
- Twenty-eight-and-a-half percent of those crimes were anti-social behavior.
- Violence and sexual offenses accounted for 28.19%.
- Other prevalent categories include vehicle crime (11.87%), theft (13.80%), and theft from the person (6.90%).

If this sounds scary, you should consider that London's crime level is moderate compared to other cities around the world, with a crime index of 53.8 and a safety index of 46.2. For context, Caracas, in Venezuela, has the highest crime index at 83.6 and Reykjavik, in Iceland, has the lowest at just 17.74.

The 10 most dangerous areas of London according to how much higher their percentage of crime was compared to the city average are City of London (762%), Westminster (213%), Kensington and Chelsea (39%), Camden (39%), Islington (22%), Southwark (14%), Hackney (14%), Hammersmith and Fulham (12%), Haringey (11%), and Lambeth (8%). Bear in mind when looking at the staggering percentages relating to the City of London and Westminster that they are also two of the busiest areas.

Comparatively, the 10 safest areas according to the percentage that they are above the London average for safety are Harrow (37%), Richmond upon Thames (37%), Bexley (33%), Sutton (32%), Kingston upon Thames (31%), Merton (29%), Bromley (28%), Barnet (27%), Wandsworth (24%), and Havering (23%).

TRAVEL TIPS AND SAFETY ADVICE

Before looking at some examples of specific emergencies that could arise and how to handle them, here are some general tips and advice to bear in mind throughout your trip:

- The drinking water in the UK is safe to drink, so there's no need to waste your spending money on the bottled stuff.
- You should never get into an unlicensed cab, or taxi with previous cases of sexual assault. Only use licensed black cabs or a taxi/Uber that you have booked in advance.
- Cabs or taxis are also safer than using public transport alone at night, although the tube and buses do tend to stay busy until much later in the evening.

- As nice as some of the attractions are at night, if visiting somewhere alone after nightfall, make sure you stick to busier places and avoid smaller roads or cut throughs. Always stay in well-lit areas.
- When out drinking, always take care of your drink, keeping it always covered or in your sight to prevent the risk of it being spiked.

Public Transport

- Bear in mind that it will be crowded, especially at peak times. My advice would be to avoid the central line on the London Underground completely between 5 p.m. and 7 p.m.
- If you insist on traveling at peak times, or don't have a choice, keep your things in your front pockets and wear your backpack on your front to deter pickpockets.
- Make sure you have your Oyster card or ticket ready as you approach the gates, as they will get busy, and creating a backlog will only cause you unnecessary stress. If you do fumble your ticket, don't worry about it—we've all been there.
- When using the escalator, use the right if you are standing and the left if you are planning on walking up and down.

- Before traveling, be sure to use the TFL app to check for any line closures or delays to prevent any wasted time or, worse, wasted Oyster credit.
- Lastly, never be afraid to ask for help! I know the tube can be intimidating and ominously quiet (for some reason, no one wants to talk), but I promise most Londoners are genuinely friendly and happy to help. Outside of that, there should be staff stationed on most platforms, or at the very least, there are help stations where you can call and talk to staff.

Street Smarts

- Beggars are common in London, particularly around busy tourist attractions and even on the London Underground (including the trains themselves). They can be aggressive out of desperation or try to tell you their sob stories. My best advice would be to only hand money over if you are comfortable and to be extra vigilant if approached at night.
- Always keep your cards secure in your bag or pockets and cover your PIN when using ATMs. Also, be careful about which ATMs you use, only using trusted banks and avoiding any that look tampered with or damaged. If you are unsure, move along to a different machine.

- The laws on drinking are more relaxed in the UK, with the legal drinking age being just 18 and cheap alcohol available on just about every street corner. As much as that might sound fun to some of you, it doesn't mean you shouldn't exercise caution, particularly younger travelers who aren't of drinking age in their home country). The last thing you want is to be heavily intoxicated in an area that you don't know very well. If you are going out for a drink, grab a licensed taxi at closing, or better yet, book your own taxi or Uber, and get yourself back to your hotel safely.
- If you are attending an event, play it safe and book yourself a ticket beforehand. London's events will be rife with ticket touts who claim to be giving you a great last-minute deal only to either sell you a ticket that's fake or that doesn't even exist in the first place. By the time you reach the turnstile, they'll be long gone with your money, I assure you, so don't risk it.
- Once you have a UK telephone number, you will be susceptible to telephone scams. They typically come in the form of a text message that asks you to phone a number to claim some kind of prize, and then they keep you on hold, so you rack up a huge phone bill. It might sound silly, but they work on lots of people, unfortunately.
- Most importantly, always keep your wits about you. If you feel uncomfortable or unsure, listen to

your gut and change route, avoid an area or person, or seek help.

The Weather

- The UK has four distinct seasons: summer, autumn, winter, and spring. These seasons can give you an idea of the kind of weather you might enjoy or endure, but the weather in the UK is very unpredictable, and it rains throughout the year.
- Be aware of the heat while traveling. Of course, this is more relevant in the summertime, but the weather in England can be unpredictable to say the least, so keep sunscreen on hand, or at least be aware of where you can pick it up in case things take a sunny turn.
- It can also get seriously cold, and not just around the winter. Pack accordingly and be aware of icy pavements and roads if the temperature plummets.

EMERGENCIES

The following are emergencies that you could face, (of course, we hope that won't be the case) and the best way to deal with them.

Lost Passport

Losing your passport in another country, and the fear of not being able to get back home, is a scary proposition for all of us! Thankfully, there are a few steps that you can follow should you manage to lose it down the back of the couch.

1. The first step is the most obvious one: look around. Think back to the last time you saw it, check behind the couch cushions, and leave no stone unturned.
2. If you come up short after your search (or know it has been stolen), then the next step is contacting your local government and reporting the loss or theft.
3. Make sure to report the loss or theft to the police too, preferably within 24 hours of it happening. The police report is important as it will be needed to make a claim with your travel insurance (if you have it).
4. If you have travel insurance, contact them as soon as possible so that they can give you any additional advice and ensure any coverage your plan provides is put in place.
5. Then, it is time to prepare the documents needed to apply for a new passport, such as an application form, passport photos, and possibly book yourself in with an interview at the passport office.

Medical Emergencies

If you get sick with something that doesn't necessarily constitute an emergency, but you want advice on medication or home remedies, the first step would be to visit one of the many pharmacies throughout London (just look for the big green plus). Pharmacists, although not doctors and unable to prescribe medication, are incredibly knowledgeable and always happy to help.

If you do have a medical emergency, rest assured that there are several hospitals that will take you in and help you regardless of whether you have a National Health Service (NHS) number or not.

Just please make sure you take out the appropriate travel and health insurance and carry your European Health Insurance Card (EHIC) if traveling from Europe.

The following hospitals have emergency rooms, meaning they'll accept and treat you if you need it.

London Welbeck Hospital

- **Address:** 27 Welbeck St, London W1G 8EN, UK
- **Contact number:** 020 7224 2242

Beckenham Beacon Urgent Care Centre

- **Address:** 379-397 Croydon Rd, Beckenham BR3 3QL, UK

- **Contact number:** 01689 863000

The Lister Hospital

- **Address:** Chelsea Bridge Rd, London SW1W 8RH, UK
- **Contact number:** 020 3811 7794

London Bridge Hospital

- **Address:** 27 Tooley St, London SE1 2PR, UK
- **Contact number:** 020 3993 8597

Royal Hospital for Neuro-Disability

- **Address:** West Hill, London SW15 3SW, UK
- **Contact number:** 020 8780 4500

North Middlesex Hospital

- **Address:** Sterling Way, London N18 1QX, UK
- **Contact number:** 020 8887 2000

Portland Hospital

- **Address:** 205-209 Great Portland St, London W1W 5AH, UK
- **Contact number:** 020 3993 4506

Priory Hospital

- **Address:** Priory Lane, Roehampton, London SW15 5JJ, UK
- **Contact number:** 020 8876 8261

The Princess Grace Hospital

- **Address:** 42-52 Nottingham Pl, London W1U 5NY, UK
- **Contact number:** 020 3811 6217

Spire St. Anthony's Hospital, London

- **Address:** 801 London Road, North Cheam, Sutton, Surrey SM3 9DW, UK
- **Contact number:** 020 8337 6691

Fitzrovia Hospital

- **Address:** 14 Fitzroy St, London W1T 6AH
- **Contact number:** 020 7034 3300

St Pancras Hospital

- **Address:** 4 St Pancras Way, London NW1 0PE
- **Contact number:** 020 3317 3500

Weymouth Street Hospital

- **Address:** 42-46 Weymouth St, London W1G 6NP
- **Contact number:** 020 7935 1200

Important Phone Numbers

- 112 or 999 is to be used for urgent police, fire, or ambulance services
- 101 is for police matters that are nonurgent
- 111 is for nonurgent medical advice

Being Robbed

Being robbed is a scary situation that affects you in more ways than just a potential loss of goods. If you are ever unfortunate enough to be in that situation, consider the following advice:

1. Firstly, remember that your belongings aren't worth serious injury, try to stay calm and resist the urge to scream for help or fight back, hand over what they are asking for and only seek help once you are either away from the culprit or back in a well-populated area.
2. Your next step should be contacting either your national embassy or high commission office for support, as well as the local police force, who will

take a description to give them the best chance of finding your attacker.

3. If your hotel keys have been stolen, notify the hotel so they can arrange a change of locks to protect you.
4. If debit or credit cards have been stolen, call your bank and get them canceled as soon as possible so they can block any future transactions (and potentially help the police).
5. The bank may also be able to help you protect your money by transferring it into a temporary account, ensuring you aren't left without any money while the theft is investigated.
6. Contact your insurance company to see what they can provide in the way of replacements and support.
7. Keep your chin up! In a busy city, the reality is that people are robbed and pickpocketed; it is an unfortunate reality of busy city life. Don't blame yourself and try to keep it from ruining your trip.

Missing the Last Tube Train

If you miss the last tube train, don't panic; head for an open takeaway or business instead of hanging around alone in the dark, and either call an Uber or taxi if you can't see any black cabs around. Another option is the bus if you are near a stop, but if it is late at night, try not to walk too far on your own if you are unsure of your surroundings.

In our last chapter, we will look at some itineraries crafted for history buffs, those who want a modern trip, travelers on a tight budget, travelers without a budget, those traveling with family, couples, and travelers who are part of the LGBTQIA+ community.

9

ITINERARIES

Discover the magic of London through perfectly crafted itineraries that take you on the journey of a lifetime. From royal palaces to hidden gems, this chapter will guide you on how to make the most of your limited time in this city and ensure that you don't miss out on anything that makes London so special.

Whether you have three days or a whole week, these itineraries will help you see London in a whole new light regardless of the types of activities and events you want to enjoy during your stay.

Just remember that these are only templates designed to inspire your own trips, so don't feel tied to anything—shuffle things around, take things out, and go nuts. This is your trip, after all.

Side note: Some date-specific events will be included in the itineraries; if they don't work logistically with your date or time of travel, just swap them out.

HISTORIC

Day Trip

Activity/event	Time	Duration	Fee ($)
Horniman Gardens	8:30 a.m.	1 hour	Free
Tower of London	10 a.m.	2 hours	43
The Houses of Parliament	12:30 p.m.	90 minutes	23
Westminster Abbey	2:30 p.m.	1 hour	35
British Museum	4 p.m.	1 hour	Free
Trafalgar Square	5:30 p.m.	1 hour	Free
The Savoy Theatre	7 p.m.	3 hours+	From 150
			Total: 251+

Three-Day Trip

Activity/event	**Time**	**Duration**	**Fee ($)**
Day 1			
Hyde Park	8 a.m.	90 minutes	Free
Tower of London	10 a.m.	2 hours	43
The Houses of Parliament	12:30 p.m.	90 minutes	23
Westminster Abbey	2:30 p.m.	2 hours	35
Tate Modern	5 p.m.	1 hour	Free
Trafalgar Square	6 p.m.	45 minutes	Free
The Savoy Theatre	7 p.m.	3 hours+	From 150
Day 2			
Horniman Gardens	9 a.m.	1 hour	Free
Horniman Museum	10 a.m.	1 hour	Free
Churchill War Rooms	11:30 a.m.	1 hour	35
Kensington Gardens	1 p.m.	1 hour	Free
Kensington Palace	2 p.m.	2 hours	33
The London Bridge Experience and London Tombs	4:30 p.m.	90 minutes	38
Hampstead Heath	6:30 p.m.	Until you get too cold!	Free

Day 3			
St. Paul's Cathedral	9 a.m.	2 hours	30
British Museum	11 a.m.	2 hours	Free
Hampton Court Palace	1:30 p.m.	2 hours	39
Buckingham Palace	4 p.m.	2 hours	43
St. James's Park	6:30 p.m.	Until you get too cold!	Free
			Total: 469+

Five-Day Trip

Activity/event	**Time**	**Duration**	**Fee ($)**
Day 1			
Hyde Park	8 a.m.	90 minutes	Free
Tower of London	10 a.m.	2 hours	43
The Houses of Parliament	12:30 p.m.	90 minutes	23
Westminster Abbey	2:30 p.m.	2 hours	35
Tate Modern	5 p.m.	1 hour	Free
Trafalgar Square	6 p.m.	45 minutes	Free
The Savoy Theatre	7 p.m.	3 hours+	From 150

Day 2			
Horniman Gardens	9 a.m.	1 hour	Free
Horniman Museum	10 a.m.	1 hour	Free
Churchill War Rooms	11:30 a.m.	1 hour	35
Kensington Gardens	1 p.m.	1 hour	Free
Kensington Palace	2 p.m.	2 hours	33
The London Bridge Experience and London Tombs	4:30 p.m.	90 minutes	38
Hampstead Heath	6:30 p.m.	Until you get too cold!	Free

Day 3			
St. Paul's Cathedral	9 a.m.	2 hours	30
British Museum	11 a.m.	2 hours	Free
Hampton Court Palace	1:30 p.m.	2 hours	39
Buckingham Palace	4 p.m.	2 hours	43
St. James's Park	6:30 p.m.	Until you get too cold!	Free

Day 4			
Tower Bridge	9:30 a.m.	90 minutes	16
Imperial War Museum	11:30 a.m.	3 hours	Free
Royal Academy of Arts	3 p.m.	1 hour	Free
Victoria and Albert Museum	4:30 p.m.	1 hour 15 minutes	Free
Battersea Park	5:45 p.m.	1 hour	Free
Jack the Ripper Tour	7:30 p.m.	1 hour 45 minutes	23

Day 5			
Abbey Road	8 a.m.	1 hour	Free
Richmond Park	9:30 a.m.	90 minutes	Free
Big Bus London Hop-On Hop-Off Tour and River Cruise	12 p.m.	3 hours	From 52
London Docklands Museum	3:30 p.m.	1 hour 30 minutes	Free
IFS Cloud Cable Car	5:15 p.m.	30 minutes	15
The Old Vic Theatre	7:30 p.m.	3 hours+	25+
			Total: 600+

Week-Long Trip

Activity/event	Time	Duration	Fee ($)
Day 1			
Hyde Park	8 a.m.	90 minutes	Free
Tower of London	10 a.m.	2 hours	43
The Houses of Parliament	12:30 p.m.	90 minutes	23
Westminster Abbey	2:30 p.m.	2 hours	35
Tate Modern	5 p.m.	1 hour	Free
Trafalgar Square	6 p.m.	45 minutes	Free
The Savoy Theatre	7 p.m.	3 hours+	From 150
Day 2			
Horniman Gardens	9 a.m.	1 hour	Free
Horniman Museum	10 a.m.	1 hour	Free
Churchill War Rooms	11:30 a.m.	1 hour	35
Kensington Gardens	1 p.m.	1 hour	Free
Kensington Palace	2 p.m.	2 hours	33
The London Bridge Experience and London Tombs	4:30 p.m.	90 minutes	38
Hampstead Heath	6:30 p.m.	Until you get too cold!	Free

Day 3			
St. Paul's Cathedral	9 a.m.	2 hours	30
British Museum	11 a.m.	2 hours	Free
Hampton Court Palace	1:30 p.m.	2 hours	39
Buckingham Palace	4 p.m.	2 hours	43
St. James's Park	6:30 p.m.	Until you get too cold!	Free

Day 4			
Tower Bridge	9:30 a.m.	90 minutes	16
Imperial War Museum	11:30 a.m.	3 hours	Free
Royal Academy of Arts	3 p.m.	1 hour	Free
Victoria and Albert Museum	4:30 p.m.	1 hour 15 minutes	Free
Battersea Park	5:45 p.m.	1 hour	Free
Jack the Ripper Tour	7:30 p.m.	1 hour 45 minutes	23

Day 5			
Abbey Road	8 a.m.	1 hour	Free
Richmond Park	9:30 a.m.	90 minutes	Free
Big Bus London Hop-On Hop-Off Tour and River Cruise	12 p.m.	3 hours	From 52
London Docklands Museum	3:30 p.m.	1 hour 30 minutes	Free
IFS Cloud Cable Car	5:15 p.m.	30 minutes	15
The Old Vic Theatre	7:30 p.m.	3 hours+	25+

Day 6			
Greenwich Park	8 a.m.	2 hours	Free
Queen's House	10 a.m.	1 hour	Free
Greenwich to Westminster Thames River Boat Tour	11:30 a.m.	1 hour	20
Covent Garden	1 p.m.	90 minutes	Free
Natural History Museum	3 p.m.	2 hours and 30 minutes	Free
Royal Albert Hall	6 p.m.	Varies	From 25

Day 7			
National Gallery	10 a.m.	4 hours	Free
Shakespeare's Globe	2:30 p.m.	45 minutes	32
London Mithraeum	3:45 p.m.	1 hour	Free
Hampstead Heath	5:30 p.m.	Until you get too cold!	Free
			Total: 677+

Fortnight Long Trip

Activity/event	**Time**	**Duration**	**Fee ($)**
Day 1			
Hyde Park	8 a.m.	90 minutes	Free
Tower of London	10 a.m.	2 hours	43
The Houses of Parliament	12:30 p.m.	90 minutes	23
Westminster Abbey	2:30 p.m.	2 hours	35
Tate Modern	5 p.m.	1 hour	Free
Trafalgar Square	6 p.m.	45 minutes	Free
The Savoy Theatre	7 p.m.	3 hours+	From 150

Day 2			
Horniman Gardens	9 a.m.	1 hour	Free
Horniman Museum	10 a.m.	1 hour	Free
Churchill War Rooms	11:30 a.m.	1 hour	35
Kensington Gardens	1 p.m.	1 hour	Free
Kensington Palace	2 p.m.	2 hours	33
The London Bridge Experience and London Tombs	4:30 p.m.	90 minutes	38
Hampstead Heath	6:30 p.m.	Until you get too cold!	Free

Day 3			
St. Paul's Cathedral	9 a.m.	2 hours	30
British Museum	11: 30 a.m.	2 hours	Free
Hampton Court Palace	2 p.m.	2 hours	39
Tate Modern	4:30 p.m.	90 minutes	Free

Day 4			
Tower Bridge	9:30 a.m.	90 minutes	16
The London Bridge Experience and London Tombs	11:30 a.m.	90 minutes	38
Imperial War Museum	1:30 p.m.	2 hours and 30 minutes	Free
Victoria and Albert Museum	4:30 p.m.	1 hour 15 minutes	Free
Battersea Park	6 p.m.	As long as you like!	Free

Day 5			
Abbey Road	8 a.m.	1 hour	Free
Richmond Park	9:30 a.m.	90 minutes	Free
Big Bus London Hop-On Hop-Off Tour and River Cruise	12 p.m.	3 hours	From 52
London Docklands Museum	3:30 p.m.	1 hour 30 minutes	Free
IFS Cloud Cable Car	5:15 p.m.	30 minutes	15
The Old Vic Theatre	7:30 p.m.	3 hours+	25+

Day 6			
Greenwich Park	8 a.m.	2 hours	Free
Queen's House	10 a.m.	1 hour	Free
Greenwich to Westminster Thames River Boat Tour	11:30 a.m.	1 hour	20
Covent Garden	1 p.m.	90 minutes	Free
Natural History Museum	3 p.m.	2 hours and 30 minutes	Free
Holland Park	6 p.m.	Until you get too cold!	Free

Day 7			
National Gallery	10 a.m.	4 hours	Free
Shakespeare's Globe	2:30 p.m.	45 minutes	32
London Mithraeum	3:45 p.m.	1 hour	Free
Royal Albert Hall	6 p.m.	Varies	From 25

Day 8			
St. Dunstan in the Park Church	8:30 a.m.	1 hour	Free
Changing of the Guard	10:45 a.m.	45 minutes	Free
London Dungeon	12 p.m.	90 minutes	43
Leicester Square	2 p.m.	1 hour	Free
Chinatown	3 p.m.	1 hour	Free
London Transport Museum	4:30 p.m.	90 minutes	Free

Day 9			
Columbia Road Flower Market	9 a.m.	4 hours	Free
Maritime Museum	1:30 p.m.	2 hours	Free
Film Museum	4 p.m.	2 hours	19
Jack the Ripper Tour	7:30 p.m.	1 hour 45 minutes	23

Day 10			
Hampstead Heath	9 a.m.	4 hours	Free
The Rock 'n' Roll Museum	2 p.m.	2 hours	Free
HMS Belfast Tour	4:30 p.m.	90 minutes	65
View from The Shard	6:30 p.m.	As long as it takes to drink it all in.	36

Day 11			
Epping Forest	9 a.m.	4 hours	Free
Royal Gunpowder Mills	1:30 p.m.	2 hours	Free
Waltham Abbey Gardens	4 p.m.	1 hour	Free
Young Vic Theatre	7:30 p.m.	2 hours+	From 13

Day 12			
London Rock Music Tour	9 a.m.	8 hours	87
Day 13			
Little Venice	9 a.m.	5 hours	Free
The Sherlock Holmes Museum	2:30 p.m.	90 minutes	20
The Wallace Collection	4 p.m.	1 hour	Free
St. James's Park	5:30 p.m.	Until you get too cold!	Free

Day 14			
Oxford/Regents Street	10 a.m.	2 hours	Free
Piccadilly Circus	12 p.m.	1 hour	Free
Royal Opera House Tour	1:30 p.m.	1 hour and 15 minutes	25
Royal Academy of Arts	3 p.m.	2 hours	Free
			Total: 1008+

MODERN

As I am sure you have already worked out, this section will provide itineraries for trips leaning toward more modern trips (although we will include some landmarks in there too).

Day Trip

Activity/event	**Time**	**Duration**	**Fee ($)**
Hyde Park	8 a.m.	1 hour	Free
Science Museum	10 a.m.	2 hours	Free
The London Eye	1 p.m.	1 hour	52
Westminster to Greenwich Thames Cruise	2:30 p.m.	1 hour	20
IFS Cloud Car	4 p.m.	30 minutes	15
Up at the O2	5:30 p.m.	90 minutes	45
			Total: 132

Three-Day Trip

Activity/event	Time	Duration	Fee ($)
Day 1			
Holland Park	8 a.m.	1 hour	Free
Science Museum	10 a.m.	2 hours	Free
The London Eye	1 p.m.	1 hour	52
Westminster to Greenwich Thames Cruise	2:30 p.m.	1 hour	20
IFS Cloud Car	4 p.m.	30 minutes	15
Up at the O2	5:30 p.m.	90 minutes	45
Day 2			
Hyde Park	8 a.m.	2 hours	Free
London Zoo	10 a.m.	3 hours	40
Sea Life London	1:30 p.m.	90 minutes	38
London Dungeon	3:15 p.m.	90 minutes	43
South Bank	5 p.m.	90 minutes	Free
BFI Southbank	7 p.m.	2 hours+	From 10

Day 3			
Platform 9¾ at Kings Cross	9 a.m.	45 minutes	Free
Harry Potter Original Locations Tour	10:30 a.m.	2 hours	26
Warner Bros. Studio Tour—The Making of Harry Potter	2 p.m.	4+ hours; it closes at 8 p.m.!	66
			Total: 355+

Five-Day Trip

Activity/event	**Time**	**Duration**	**Fee ($)**
Day 1			
Holland Park	8 a.m.	1 hour	Free
Science Museum	10 a.m.	3 hours	Free
Westminster to Greenwich Thames Cruise	2:30 p.m.	1 hour	20
IFS Cloud Car	4 p.m.	30 minutes	15
Up at the O2	5:30 p.m.	90 minutes	45

Day 2			
Hyde Park	8 a.m.	2 hours	Free
London Zoo	10 a.m.	3 hours	40
Sea Life London	1:30 p.m.	90 minutes	38
London Dungeon	3:15 p.m.	90 minutes	43
London South Bank	5 p.m.	2 hours	Free
BFI Southbank	7 p.m.	2 hours+	From 10

Day 3			
Platform 9¾ at Kings Cross	9 a.m.	45 minutes	Free
Harry Potter Original Locations Tour	10:30 a.m.	2 hours	26
Warner Bros. Studio Tour—The Making of Harry Potter.	2 p.m.	4+ hours; it closes at 8 p.m.!	66

Day 4			
Wembley Stadium Tour	10 a.m.	2 hours	31
Wembley Park	12 p.m.	1 hour	Free
Olympic Park Tour	2:30 p.m.	90 minutes	25
ArcelorMittal Orbit	4 p.m.	1 hour	25
Westfields Shopping Center	5:15 p.m.	90 minutes	That's up to you!
Theater Royal Stratford East	7:30 p.m.	2 hours+	From 30

Day 5			
Regent's Park	9 a.m.	45 minutes	Free
Madame Tussauds	10 a.m.	2 hours	46
Tate Modern	1 p.m.	90 minutes	Free
Borough Market	3 p.m.	2 hours	Free
View from The Shard	5:30 p.m.	As long as you like!	36
			Total: 548

Week-Long Trip

Activity/event	**Time**	**Duration**	**Fee ($)**
Day 1			
Holland Park	8 a.m.	1 hour	Free
Science Museum	10 a.m.	2 hours	Free
The London Eye	1 p.m.	1 hour	52
Westminster to Greenwich Thames Cruise	2:30 p.m.	1 hour	20
IFS Cloud Car	4 p.m.	30 minutes	15
Up at the O2	5:30 p.m.	90 minutes	45

Day 2			
Hyde Park	8 a.m.	2 hours	Free
London Zoo	10 a.m.	3 hours	40
Sea Life London	1:30 p.m.	90 minutes	38
London Dungeon	3:15 p.m.	90 minutes	43
South Bank	5 p.m.	90 minutes	Free
BFI Southbank	7 p.m.	2 hours+	From 10

Day 3			
Platform 9¾ at Kings Cross	9 a.m.	45 minutes	Free
Harry Potter Original Locations Tour	10:30 a.m.	2 hours	26
Warner Bros. Studio Tour—The Making of Harry Potter	2 p.m.	4+ hours; it closes at 8 p.m.!	66

Day 4			
Wembley Stadium Tour	10 a.m.	2 hours	31
Wembley Park	12 p.m.	1 hour	Free
Olympic Park Tour	2:30 p.m.	90 minutes	25
ArcelorMittal Orbit	4 p.m.	1 hour	25
Westfields Shopping Center	5:15 p.m.	90 minutes	That's up to you!
Theater Royal Stratford East	7:30 p.m.	2 hours+	From 30

Day 5			
Regent's Park	9 a.m.	45 minutes	Free
Madame Tussauds	10 a.m.	2 hours	46
Tate Modern	1 p.m.	90 minutes	Free
Borough Market	3 p.m.	2 hours	Free
View from The Shard	5:30 p.m.	As long as you like!	36

Day 6			
Shoreditch	9 a.m.	4 hours	Free
Camden	2 p.m.	4 hours	Free
Barbican Conservatory	6:30 p.m.	1 hour	Free
Barbican Center	8 p.m.	2 hours+	From 20

Day 7			
Covent Garden	10 a.m.	90 minutes	Free
Leicester Square	12 p.m.	90 minutes	Free
M & M World	1:30 p.m.	1 hour	Free
The Lego Store	2:45 p.m.	1 hour	Free
Chinatown	4 p.m.	90 minutes	Free
Piccadilly Circus	6 p.m.	1 hour	Free
Jack the Ripper Tour	7:30 p.m.	1 hour 45 minutes	23
			Total: 591+

Fortnight Long Trip

Activity/event	Time	Duration	Fee ($)
Day 1			
Holland Park	8 a.m.	1 hour	Free
Science Museum	10 a.m.	2 hours	Free
The London Eye	1 p.m.	1 hour	52
Westminster to Greenwich Thames Cruise	2:30 p.m.	1 hour	20
IFS Cloud Car	4 p.m.	30 minutes	15
Up at the O2	5:30 p.m.	90 minutes	45
Day 2			
Hyde Park	8 a.m.	2 hours	Free
London Zoo	10 a.m.	3 hours	40
Sea Life London	1:30 p.m.	90 minutes	38
London Dungeon	3:15 p.m.	90 minutes	43
South Bank	5 p.m.	90 minutes	Free
BFI Southbank	7 p.m.	2 hours+	From 10

Day 3			
Platform 9¾ at Kings Cross	9 a.m.	45 minutes	Free
Harry Potter Original Locations Tour	10:30 a.m.	2 hours	26
Warner Bros. Studio Tour—The Making of Harry Potter.	2 p.m.	4+ hours; it closes at 8 p.m.!	66

Day 4			
Wembley Stadium Tour	10 a.m.	2 hours	31
Wembley Park	12 p.m.	1 hour	Free
Olympic Park Tour	2:30 p.m.	90 minutes	25
ArcelorMittal Orbit	4 p.m.	1 hour	25
Westfields Shopping Center	5:15 p.m.	90 minutes	That's up to you!
Theater Royal Stratford East	7:30 p.m.	2 hours+	From 30

Day 5			
Regent's Park	9 a.m.	45 minutes	Free
Madame Tussauds	10 a.m.	2 hours	46
Tate Modern	1 p.m.	90 minutes	Free
Borough Market	3 p.m.	2 hours	Free
View from The Shard	5:30 p.m.	As long as you like!	36

Day 6			
Shoreditch	9 a.m.	4 hours	Free
Camden	2 p.m.	4 hours	Free
Barbican Conservatory	6:30 p.m.	1 hour	Free
Barbican Center	8 p.m.	2 hours+	From 20

Day 7			
Covent Garden	10 a.m.	90 minutes	Free
Leicester Square	12 p.m.	90 minutes	Free
M & M World	1:30 p.m.	1 hour	Free
The Lego Store	2:45 p.m.	1 hour	Free
Chinatown	4 p.m.	90 minutes	Free

Day 8			
London Rock Music Tour	9 a.m.	8 hours	87
Sky Garden	6 p.m.	As long as you like!	Free
Day 9			
The London Bridge Experience and London Tombs	11 a.m.	90 minutes	38
The Rock 'n' Roll Museum	1 p.m.	2 hours	Free
Film museum	3:30 p.m.	2 hours	19
Public Viewing Gallery at Oxo Tower	6 p.m.	As long as you like!	Free

Day 10			
Carnaby Street	10 a.m.	3 hours	Free
Photographer's Gallery	1:30 p.m.	1 hour	Free
Trafalgar Square	2 p.m.	2 hours	Free
National Gallery	4:15 p.m.	1 hour and 45 minutes	Free
Charing Cross Theatre	7:30 p.m.	2 hours+	From 23

Day 11			
Borough Market	10 a.m.	4 hours	Free
London Dungeon	2 p.m.	90 minutes	43
Jubilee Gardens	4 p.m.	1 hour	Free
The London Eye	5:30 p.m.	1 hour	52

Day 12			
Little Venice	9 a.m.	4 hours and 30 minutes	Free
Lord's Cricket Ground Tour	2 p.m.	100 minutes	39
The Sherlock Holmes Museum	4 p.m.	90 minutes	20
Regents Park	5:45 p.m.	1 hour	Free
Regents Park Open Air Theatre	7:45 p.m.	2 hours and 30 minutes	From 70

Regents Park Open Air Theatre	7:45 p.m.	2 hours and 30 minutes	From 70
Day 13			
Epping Forest	9 a.m.	5 hours	Free
Hampstead Heath	3 p.m.	4 hours	Free
Day 14			
Battersea Park	9 a.m.	3 hours	Free
Saatchi Gallery	12:30 p.m.	90 minutes	32
Battersea Power Station	2:30 p.m.	3 hours	Free
Ride the Thames Clipper from Battersea Power Station back to the city center to see the lights!	6 p.m.	45 minutes	11
			Total: 1025+

FREE

I know this sounds too good to be true, but it isn't! Next, we will offer a range of itineraries that are filled with only free attractions for those of you on a strict budget (or who just love the word *free* as much as we do).

Day Trip

Activity/event	Time	Duration	Fee ($)
Hyde Park	8 a.m.	2 hours	Free
National History Museum	10:30 a.m.	2 hours	Free
Russell Square	1 p.m.	1 hour	Free
British Museum	2:30 p.m.	2 hours	Free
St. Dunstan in the East Church Garden	5 p.m.	1 hour	Free
Sky Garden	6 p.m.	As long as you like!	Free

Three-Day Trip

Activity/event	Time	Duration	Fee ($)
Day 1			
National History Museum	10 a.m.	2 hours	Free
Science Museum	12:15 p.m.	2 hours	Free
Victoria and Albert Museum	2:30 p.m.	2 hours	Free
St. Dunstan in the East Church Garden	5 p.m.	1 hour	Free
Sky Garden	6 p.m.	As long as you like!	Free
Day 2			
Vauxhall Pleasure Gardens	9 a.m.	45 minutes	Free
Tate Britain	10 a.m.	2 hours	Free
St. James's Park	12:15 p.m.	2 hours	Free
Tate Modern	2:30 p.m.	2 hours	Free
Viewing Platform at Oxo Tower	5 p.m.	1 hour	Free

Day 3			
Trafalgar Square	9 a.m.	1 hour	Free
The National Gallery	10 a.m.	3 hours	Free
Leicester Square	1:30 p.m.	1 hour	Free
Chinatown	2:30 p.m.	1 hour	Free
London Mithraeum	4 p.m.	1 hour	Free
St. Paul's Cathedral	5:30 p.m.	As long as you like!	Free

Five-Day Trip

Activity/event	**Time**	**Duration**	**Fee ($)**
Day 1			
National History Museum	10 a.m.	3 hours	Free
Science Museum	1:15 p.m.	3 hours	Free
St. Dunstan in the East Church Garden	4:30 p.m.	1 hour	Free
Sky Garden	6 p.m.	As long as you like!	Free

Day 2			
Vauxhall Pleasure Gardens	9 a.m.	45 minutes	Free
Tate Britain	10 a.m.	2 hours	Free
St. James's Park	12:15 p.m.	2 hours	Free
Tate Modern	2:30 p.m.	2 hours	Free
Viewing Platform at Oxo Tower	5 p.m.	1 hour	Free

Day 3			
Trafalgar Square	9 a.m.	1 hour	Free
The National Gallery	10 a.m.	3 hours	Free
Leicester Square	1:30 p.m.	1 hour	Free
Chinatown	2:30 p.m.	1 hour	Free
London Mithraeum	4 p.m.	1 hour	Free
St. Paul's Cathedral	5:30 p.m.	As long as you like!	Free

Day 4			
Greenwich Park	9 a.m.	2 hours	Free
Queen's House Museum	11 a.m.	90 minutes	Free
National Maritime Museum	12:45 p.m.	2 hours	Free
Greenwich Market	3 p.m.	2 and a half hours	Free
O2 Arena	6 p.m.	As long as you like, it closes at 11 p.m.!	Free

Day 5			
Royal Academy of Arts	10 a.m.	3 hours	Free
The Photographers Gallery	1:15 p.m.	1 hour	Free
The Wallace Collection	2:30 p.m.	2 hours	Free
Regent's Park	5 p.m.	As long as you like!	Free

Week-Long Trip

Activity/event	**Time**	**Duration**	**Fee ($)**
Day 1			
National History Museum	10 a.m.	2 hours	Free
Science Museum	12:15 p.m.	2 hours	Free
Victoria and Albert Museum	2:30 p.m.	2 hours	Free
St. Dunstan in the East Church Garden	5 p.m.	1 hour	Free
Sky Garden	6 p.m.	As long as you like!	Free

Day 2			
Vauxhall Pleasure Gardens	9 a.m.	45 minutes	Free
Tate Britain	10 a.m.	2 hours	Free
St. James's Park	12:15 p.m.	2 hours	Free
Tate Modern	2:30 p.m.	2 hours	Free
Viewing Platform at Oxo Tower	5 p.m.	1 hour	Free

Day 3			
Trafalgar Square	9 a.m.	1 hour	Free
The National Gallery	10 a.m.	3 hours	Free
Leicester Square	1:30 p.m.	1 hour	Free
Chinatown	2:30 p.m.	1 hour	Free
London Mithraeum	4 p.m.	1 hour	Free
St. Paul's Cathedral	5:30 p.m.	As long as you like!	Free

Day 4			
Greenwich Park	9 a.m.	2 hours	Free
Queen's House Museum	11 a.m.	90 minutes	Free
National Maritime Museum	12:45 p.m.	2 hours	Free
Greenwich Market	3 p.m.	2 hours and 30 minutes	Free
O2 Arena	6 p.m.	As long as you like, it closes at 11 p.m.!	Free

Day 5			
Royal Academy of Arts	10 a.m.	3 hours	Free
The Photographers Gallery	1:15 p.m.	2 hours	Free
The Wallace Collection	3:30 p.m.	2 hours	Free
Regent's Park	5 p.m.	As long as you like!	Free

Day 6			
Little Venice	9 a.m.	5 hours	Free
Serpentine Gallery	2:30 p.m.	2 hours	Free
The Design Museum	5 p.m.	1 hour	Free
Holland Park	6 p.m.	As long as you like!	Free

Day 7			
Belgravia Square	9 a.m.	45 minutes	Free
Changing of the Guard (from the Buckingham Palace gates)	10:45 a.m.	1 hour	Free
Westminster Bridge for sightseeing	12:15 p.m.	1 hour	Free
Imperial War Museum	1:15 p.m.	3 hours	Free
Arch Bishop's Park	4:45 p.m.	As long as you like!	Free

Fortnight Long Trip

Activity/event	Time	Duration	Fee ($)
Day 1			
National History Museum	10 a.m.	2 hours	Free
Science Museum	12:15 p.m.	2 hours	Free
Victoria and Albert Museum	2:30 p.m.	2 hours	Free
St. Dunstan in the East Church Garden	5 p.m.	1 hour	Free
Sky Garden	6 p.m.	As long as you like!	Free
Day 2			
Vauxhall Pleasure Gardens	9 a.m.	45 minutes	Free
Tate Britain	10 a.m.	2 hours	Free
St. James's Park	12:15 p.m.	2 hours	Free
Tate Modern	2:30 p.m.	2 hours	Free
Viewing Platform at Oxo Tower	5 p.m.	1 hour	Free

Day 3			
Trafalgar Square	9 a.m.	1 hour	Free
The National Gallery	10 a.m.	3 hours	Free
Leicester Square	1:30 p.m.	1 hour	Free
Chinatown	2:30 p.m.	1 hour	Free
London Mithraeum	4 p.m.	1 hour	Free
St. Paul's Cathedral	5:30 p.m.	As long as you like!	Free

Day 4			
Greenwich Park	9 a.m.	2 hours	Free
Queen's House Museum	11 a.m.	90 minutes	Free
National Maritime Museum	12:45 p.m.	2 hours	Free
Greenwich Market	3 p.m.	2 hours and 30 minutes	Free
O2 Arena	6 p.m.	As long as you like, it closes at 11 p.m.!	Free

Day 5			
Royal Academy of Arts	10 a.m.	3 hours	Free
The Photographers Gallery	1:15 p.m.	1 hour	Free
The Wallace Collection	2:30 p.m.	2 hours	Free
Regent's Park	5 p.m.	As long as you like!	Free

Day 6			
Little Venice	9 a.m.	5 hours	Free
Serpentine Gallery	2:30 p.m.	2 hours	Free
The Design Museum	5 p.m.	1 hour	Free
Holland Park	6 p.m.	As long as you like!	Free

Day 7			
Belgravia Square	9 a.m.	45 minutes	Free
Changing of the Guard (from the Buckingham Palace gates).	10:45 a.m.	1 hour	Free
Westminster Bridge for sightseeing	12:15 p.m.	1 hour	Free
Imperial War Museum	1:15 p.m.	3 hours	Free
St. James's Park	4:15 p.m.	As long as you like!	Free

Day 8			
Platform 9¾	9 a.m.	1 hour	Free
Columbia Road Flower Market	10:30 a.m.	4 hours	Free
Haggerston Park	3 p.m.	2 hours	Free
Bethnal Green	5 p.m. onwards	As long as you like!	Free

Day 9			
Horniman Gardens	9 a.m.	1 hour	Free
Horniman Museum	10 a.m.	2 hours	Free
Wellcome Collection	12 p.m.	90 minutes	Free
Whitechapel Gallery	2 p.m.	2 hours	Free
Old Spitalfields Market	4:30 p.m.	As long as you like, it closes at 8 p.m.!	Free

Day 10			
Finsbury Circus Gardens	9 a.m.	30 minutes	Free
Guildhall Town Hall (for sightseeing)	9:45 a.m.	30 minutes	Free
Guildhall Art Gallery	10:30 a.m.	90 minutes	Free
Bank of England Museum	12:30 p.m.	2 hours	Free
Leadenhall Market	3 p.m.	2 hours	Free
St. Dunstan in the East Church Garden	5:30 p.m.	As long as you like!	Free

Day 11			
Museum of London Docklands	10 a.m.	3 hours	Free
Promenade Canary Wharf	1:15 p.m.	1 hour	Free
Canary Wharf Thames Path	2:45 p.m.	2 hours	Free
Sugar Quay Jetty	5 p.m.	As long as you like!	Free
Day 12			
Shoreditch	9 a.m.	4 hours	Free
Camden	1:30 p.m.	4 hours	Free
Barbican Conservatory	6 p.m.	30 minutes	Free

Day 13			
Kensington Park	10 a.m.	2 hours	Free
Battersea Park	1 p.m.	3 hours	
Battersea Power Station	4:30 p.m.	As long as you like, it closes at 9 p.m.!	Free
Day 14			
Epping Forest	9 a.m.	5 hours	Free
Hampstead Heath	3 p.m.	As long as you like!	Free

LGBTQIA+

The last set of itineraries will include both modern and historical activities, with a distinctly LGBTQIA+ flavor to ensure you see all the key sights and experience the best that gay London has to offer.

Day Trip

Activity/event	Time	Duration	Fee ($)
Admiral Duncan Memorial	9:30 a.m.	45 minutes	Free
Gay's the Word	11 a.m.	2 hours	Free
Queer Britain	1:30 p.m.	90 minutes	Free
Bishopsgate Institute	3:30 p.m.	1 hour	Free
Market Place Vauxhall	5 p.m.	2 hours	Free
Above the Stag	7:30 p.m.	2 hours	25
			Total: 25

Three-Day Trip

For the other itineraries, we are going to make the bold assumption that you may be in town for London Pride (July) and incorporate accordingly.

Activity/event	Time	Duration	Fee ($)
Day 1			
Admiral Duncan Memorial	9:30 a.m.	45 minutes	Free
Gay's the Word	11 a.m.	2 hours	Free
Queer Britain	1:30 p.m.	90 minutes	Free
Bishopsgate Institute	3:30 p.m.	1 hour	Free
Market Place Vauxhall	5 p.m.	2 hours	Free
Above the Stag	7:30 p.m.	2 hours	25

Day 2			
Kensington Gardens	10 a.m.	1 hour and 45 minutes	Free
London Pride	12 p.m.	6 hours	Free
The London Eye	6:30 p.m.	1 hour	52

Day 3			
Covent Garden	9 a.m.	90 minutes	Free
A Queer History of London	11 a.m.	2 hours	Free
LGBTQ Historical Virtual Tour through Soho	1:30 p.m.	4 hours	Free
Comptons of Soho	6 p.m.	As long as you like!	As much as you like!
			Total: 77+

Five-Day Trip

Activity/event	**Time**	**Duration**	**Fee ($)**
Day 1			
Admiral Duncan Memorial	9:30 a.m.	45 minutes	Free
Gay's the Word	11 a.m.	2 hours	Free
Queer Britain	1:30 p.m.	90 minutes	Free
Bishopsgate Institute	3:30 p.m.	1 hour	Free
Market Place Vauxhall	5 p.m.	As long as you like, it closes at 11 p.m.!	Free

Day 2			
Kensington Gardens	10 a.m.	1 hour and 45 minutes	Free
London Pride	12 p.m.	6 hours	Free
The London Eye	6:30 p.m.	1 hour	52
Day 3			
Covent Garden	9 a.m.	90 minutes	Free
A Queer History of London	11 a.m.	2 hours	Free
LGBTQ Historical Virtual Tour through Soho	1:30 p.m.	4 hours	Free
Comptons of Soho	6 p.m.	As long as you like!	As much as you like!

Day 4			
Vauxhall	9 a.m.	5 hours	Free
Above the Stag	2:30 p.m.	2 hours	25
Royal Vauxhall Tavern	5 p.m.	As long as you like!	As much as you like!
Day 5			
Theatreland Walking Tour	10 a.m.	4 hours	256
Shoreditch	2:30 p.m.	2 hours	Free
The Queen Adelaide	5 p.m.	90 minutes	As much as you like!
Shoreditch Town Hall	7:30 p.m.	2 hours+	From 20
			Total: 378+

Week-Long Trip

Activity/event	Time	Duration	Fee ($)
Day 1			
Horniman Gardens	9 a.m.	1 hour	Free
Horniman Museum	10 a.m.	1 hour	Free
Tower of London	11:30 a.m.	2 hours	43
Admiral Duncan Memorial	2 p.m.	45 minutes	Free
Gay's the Word	3 p.m.	2 hours	Free
Market Place Vauxhall	5:15 p.m.	As long as you like, it closes at 11 p.m.!	Free
Day 2			
Kensington Gardens	10 a.m.	1 hour and 45 minutes	Free
London Pride	12 p.m.	6 hours	Free
The London Eye	6:30 p.m.	1 hour	52
Day 3			
Covent Garden	9 a.m.	90 minutes	Free
A Queer History of London	11 a.m.	2 hours	Free
LGBTQ Historical Virtual Tour through Soho	1:30 p.m.	4 hours	Free
Comptons of Soho	6 p.m.	As long as you like!	As much as you like!

Day 4			
Vauxhall	9 a.m.	5 hours	Free
Above the Stag	2:30 p.m.	2 hours	25
Royal Vauxhall Tavern.	5 p.m.	As long as you like!	As much as you like!
Day 5			
Theatreland Walking Tour	10 a.m.	4 hours	256
Shoreditch	2:30 p.m.	4 hours	Free
The Queen Adelaide	5 p.m.	90 minutes	As much as you like!
Shoreditch Town Hall	7:30 p.m.	2 hours+	From 20

Day 6			
Westminster Abbey	9:30 a.m.	1 hour	35
The Houses of Parliament	11 a.m.	90 minutes	23
Queer Britain	1 p.m.	2 hours	Free
Bishopsgate Institute	3:30 p.m.	1 hour	Free
Spitalfields Market	5 p.m.	2 hours	Free
Watermans Arts Centre	7:30 p.m.	90 minutes+	From 15

Day 7			
Kensington Gardens	10 a.m.	2 hours	Free
Kensington Palace	12 p.m.	2 hours	33
Buckingham Palace	2:30 p.m.	2 hours	43
Leicester Square	5 p.m.	1 hour	Free
Chinatown	6 p.m.	90 minutes	Free
Rupert Street Bar	8 p.m.	As long as you like!	As much as you like!
			Total: 527+

LGBTQ Historical Virtual Tour through Soho

Fortnight Long Trip

Activity/event	**Time**	**Duration**	**Fee ($)**
Day 1			
Horniman Gardens	9 a.m.	1 hour	Free
Horniman Museum	10 a.m.	1 hour	Free
Tower of London	11:30 a.m.	2 hours	43
Admiral Duncan Memorial	2 p.m.	45 minutes	Free
Gay's the Word	3 p.m.	2 hours	Free
Market Place Vauxhall	5:15 p.m.	As long as you like, it closes at 11 p.m.!	Free

Day 2			
Kensington Gardens	10 a.m.	1 hour and 45 minutes	Free
London Pride	12 p.m.	6 hours	Free
The London Eye	6:30 p.m.	1 hour	52
Day 3			
Covent Garden	9 a.m.	90 minutes	Free
A Queer History of London	11 a.m.	2 hours	Free
LGBTQ Historical Virtual Tour through Soho	1:30 p.m.	4 hours	Free
Comptons of Soho	6 p.m.	As long as you like!	As much as you like!

Day 4			
Vauxhall	9 a.m.	5 hours	Free
Above the Stag	2:30 p.m.	2 hours	25
Royal Vauxhall Tavern.	5 p.m.	As long as you like!	As much as you like!
Day 5			
Theatreland Walking Tour	10 a.m.	4 hours	256
Shoreditch	2:30 p.m.	4 hours	Free
The Queen Adelaide	5 p.m.	90 minutes	As much as you like!
Shoreditch Town Hall	7:30 p.m.	2 hours+	From 20

Day 6			
Westminster Abbey	9:30 a.m.	1 hour	35
The Houses of Parliament	11 a.m.	90 minutes	23
Queer Britain	1 p.m.	2 hours	Free
Bishopsgate Institute	3:30 p.m.	1 hour	Free
Spitalfields Market	5 p.m.	2 hours	Free
Watermans Arts Centre	7:30 p.m.	90 minutes+	From 15

Day 7			
Kensington Gardens	10 a.m.	2 hours	Free
Kensington Palace	12 p.m.	2 hours	33
Buckingham Palace	2:30 p.m.	2 hours	43
Leicester Square	5 p.m.	1 hour	Free
Chinatown	6 p.m.	90 minutes	Free
Rupert Street Bar	8 p.m.	As long as you like!	As much as you like!

Day 8			
The Green Park	9 a.m.	2 hours	Free
The London of Oscar Wilde Tour	11 a.m.	2 hours	11.50
Hyde Park	1:15 p.m.	1 hour	Free
Madame Tussauds	2:45 p.m.	2 hours	46
G-A-Y Bar	5:15 p.m.	As long as you like!	As much as you like!

Day 9			
Little Venice	9 a.m.	5 hours	Free
Trafalgar Square	2:30 p.m.	1 hour	Free
The National Gallery	3:30 p.m.	2 hours and 30 minutes	Free
The Harold Pinter Theatre	7:30 p.m.	2 hours and 30 minutes	From 20

Day 10			
British Museum	10 a.m.	4 hours	Free
The London Eye	2:30 p.m.	1 hour	52
Westminster to Greenwich Thames Cruise	3:45 p.m.	1 hour	20
IFS Cloud Car	5 p.m.	30 minutes	15
Greenwich Park	5:45 p.m.	2 hours	Free
The George and Dragon	8 p.m.	As long as you like!	As much as you like!

Day 11			
Columbia Road Flower Market	9 a.m.	4 hours	Free
Maritime Museum	1:30 p.m.	2 hours	Free
Film Museum	4 p.m.	2 hours	19
The Star Liverpool Street	7 p.m.	As long as you like!	As much as you like!

Day 12			
Oxford/Regents Street	10 a.m.	2 hours	Free
Piccadilly Circus	12 p.m.	1 hour	Free
Royal Opera House Tour	1:30 p.m.	1 hour and 15 minutes	25
Royal Academy of Arts	3 p.m.	2 hours	Free
Freedom Bar.	5:30 p.m.	As long as you like!	As much as you like!

Day 13			
Epping Forest	9 a.m.	5 hours	Free
Hampstead Heath	3 p.m.	4 hours	Free
Day 14			
Oxford/Regents Street	10 a.m.	3 hours	Free (minus all the shopping you will be doing, of course!).
Carnaby Street	1:15 p.m.	90 minutes	See above!
Royal Opera House Tour	3 p.m.	1 hour and 15 minutes	25
Piccadilly Circus	4:30 p.m.	1 hour and 15 minutes	Free
The Yard Bar	6 p.m.	Up until your train leaves!	As much as you like!
			Total: 760.50+

A Word of Advice

Most of the activities and events on all the itineraries will require booking ahead (even those that are free), so don't forget to take your chosen itinerary, tweak it, and get booking (in some cases you will save money too!).

RELEVANT LINKS

For effortless navigation through the heart of London, simply simply scan the QR code to access clickable links to all your favorite spots. Say goodbye to cumbersome folding maps—our digital portal puts London's best attractions right at your fingertips. Scan, click, and explore—the city's iconic landmarks, hidden gems, and local favorites are just a tap away!

Follow us on:

- Instagram: www.instagram.com/worldofwunderers/
- Facebook: www.facebook.com/worldofwunder
- "X" Formerly known as Twitter: twitter.com/worldofwunderer
- Website: www.worldofwunder.com

SHARE THE ADVENTURE!

You'll never be done with exploring London, and we hope you leave with the wish to return. With such an exciting adventure ahead, take a moment to spread the travel bug!

Simply by sharing your honest opinion of this book and a little about your own travels, you'll make it easy for other adventurers to find the insights they're looking for.

SO, HOW DID WE DO?

Thank you so much for your support. May the world be your oyster (card)!

CONCLUSION

Phew! What a journey!

We here at World of Wunder hope that this guide can provide an invaluable tool that helps ensure you travel at the right time of year, stay in the right place, and maximize every minute that you spend in London.

But above all else, we hope you prioritize your safety!

Go ride a rickshaw through busy Leicester Square, stare in awe at Westminster Palace from the dizzy heights of the London Eye, and shuffle into the central line with a sweaty smile because you know your destination is worth the squeeze.

Westminster Palace at night

London is a stunning city, and we are sure you will have a trip that you won't soon forget! Just watch the roads, ask for help when needed, and keep your money, cards, and wits about you always.

The best part is that even with this treasure trove of information, there is no way you will cover everything London has to offer: doing so in one, or even five, trips is an insurmountable task.

We challenge you to search for your own hidden gems and drop them in the review or comment section where you found us to help other travelers (and us, of course).

Stay safe, have fun, and happy travels.

We will see you for the next World of Wunder travel guide!

ABOUT THE AUTHOR

Meet the intrepid minds behind World of Wunder, where exploration meets expertise in the world of travel. Our guidebook series isn't just about mapping out destinations; it's a passionate ode to wanderlust—a testament to the insatiable curiosity to explore the world. Each author is a local luminary, a beacon illuminating the lesser-known marvels, the hidden gems, and the off-the-beaten-path wonders of their home.

But what exactly is 'Wunder'? It's more than just a word—it's a celebration of wanderlust, encapsulating the enthusiasm and thrill of discovery. Our authors embody this spirit, infusing their narratives with a blend of cultural insight, historical anecdotes, and personal tales that paint a vivid portrait of their locale.

In our guides, expect to traverse uncharted territories, unraveling the secrets tucked away from the mainstream tourist trail. From secluded villages with centuries-old traditions to breathtaking natural vistas that defy description, our authors invite you to delve deeper, urging you to savor the untamed essence of a destination.

We take pride in uncovering the pulse of local life—sharing the locals' favorite haunts for gastronomic delights, the tucked-away eateries serving authentic cuisine, and the hidden bars pouring concoctions known only to the savviest of residents. Food and drink aren't just sustenance; they're gateways to cultural understanding, and our guides ensure you savor every nuance.

World of Wunder isn't for the casual traveler—it's crafted for the enterprising adventurer, the seeker of authenticity, the one who craves experiences beyond the ordinary. Whether you're an avid backpacker, a cultural enthusiast, or simply someone hungry for the extraordinary, our guides are your passport to the uncharted realms of discovery. Let the journey begin!

REFERENCES

About Hammersmith. (n.d.). Hammersmith BID. https://hammersmithbid.co.uk/about-hammersmith/

About us | Covent Garden. (n.d.). Covent Garden London. https://www.coventgarden.london/about-us/#:~:text=Covent%20Garden%20is%20a%20world

Abrahams, L. (2020, September 12). *The insider guide to Bloomsbury*. CN Traveller. https://www.cntraveller.com/gallery/bloomsbury-london

admin. (2021, September 13). *The best pop clubs in London*. Noisy Kitchen. https://noisykitchen.com/2021/09/13/the-best-pop-clubs-in-london/

Alexandra Palace fireworks festival 2023. (n.d.). London Cheapo. https://londoncheapo.com/events/alexandra-palace-fireworks-festival/

Amos, A. J. (2022, June 16). *Best things to do in Muswell Hill, London*. London X London. https://www.londonxlondon.com/things-to-do-muswell-hill/

Anastasiya. (2020, April 9). *Houses of Parliament facts: #14 facts about Houses of Parliament*. Montcalm London City Blog. https://www.themontcalmlondoncity.co.uk/blog/14-fun-facts-about-the-houses-of-parliament/

Andina Spitalfields | Restaurants in Shoreditch, London. (2013, December 5). Time Out London. https://www.timeout.com/london/restaurants/andina-shoreditch

ArcelorMittal Orbit tickets, products, bundles, membership plans, gift vouchers—buy online. (n.d.-a). Arcelormittalorbit. Retrieved July 27, 2023, from https://arcelormittalorbit.digitickets.co.uk/tickets

Bailey, C. (2018, February 2). *Top 10 facts about The Changing Of The Guard ceremony*. Guide London. https://www.guidelondon.org.uk/blog/british-monarchy/top-10-facts-changing-guard-ceremony/

Barber, S. (2019, May 23). *Things to do in Shoreditch, London*. CN Traveller. https://www.cntraveller.com/gallery/shoreditch-things-to-do

Barber, S. (2021, May 1). *Things to do in Hackney Central: A local's guide.* CN Traveller. https://www.cntraveller.com/gallery/things-to-do-hackney-central

Barnaby, J. (2019, September 11). *43 London quotes that say everything you need to know.* London X London. https://www.londonxlondon.com/london-quotes/#:~:text=It%20is%20similarly%20convoluted%20and

Barnaby, J. (2019, September 12). *56 weird and wonderful facts about London I'll bet you never knew.* London X London. https://www.londonxlondon.com/facts-about-london/

Barnaby, A. J. (2020, March 1). *15 cool things to do in Camden.* London X London. https://www.londonxlondon.com/things-to-do-in-camden/

Barnaby, A. J. (2022a, January 26). *32 free things to do in London—cool, fun and totally Free.* London X London. https://www.londonxlondon.com/free-things-to-do-in-london/

Barnaby, A. J. (2022b, June 23). *20+ best things to do in Covent Garden.* London X London. https://www.londonxlondon.com/things-to-do-covent-garden/

Barnaby, Julianna. "43 London Quotes That Pretty Much Say It All..." London X London. Last modified May 12, 2020. https://www.londonxlondon.com/london-quotes/.

Barzey, Ursula P. (2015, July 17). *11 facts about Westminster Abbey in London.* Guide London. https://www.guidelondon.org.uk/blog/major-london-sites/11-facts-about-westminster-abbey/

The Belgravia Hotel. (n.d.). Tripadvisor. Retrieved July 27, 2023, from https://www.tripadvisor.co.uk/Hotel_Review-g186338-d305562-Reviews-The_Belgravia_Hotel-London_England.html

Best hospitals in UK for visitors and expatriates. (n.d.). International Citizens Insurance. Retrieved July 27, 2023, from https://www.internationalinsurance.com/hospitals/uk/

The best karaoke bars, clubs and pubs in London. (2022, November 17). Time Out London. https://www.timeout.com/london/nightlife/best-karaoke-bars-in-london

The best rock music venues in London. (2023, January 21). Strawberry

Tours. https://strawberrytours.com/the-best-rock-music-venues-in-london

The best times to visit London's attractions. (2014, December 3). Londonist. https://londonist.com/2014/12/the-best-times-to-visit-londons-attractions

Best things to do in Bloomsbury, London: Area guide. (2021, July 5). London X London. https://www.londonxlondon.com/london-area-guides/bloomsbury/

Best things to do in Highgate: An insider's area guide. (2020, September 19). London X London. https://www.londonxlondon.com/london-area-guides/highgate/

Best things to do in Primrose Hill, London: Insider's area guide. (2020, September 25). London X London. https://www.londonxlondon.com/london-area-guides/primrose-hill/

Best things to do in Wimbledon, London: Insider's guide. (2021, November 22). London X London. https://www.londonxlondon.com/london-area-guides/wimbledon/

The best vegan-friendly restaurants in London. (n.d.). Time Out London. https://www.timeout.com/london/restaurants/the-best-vegan-restaurants-in-london

Bethnal Green area guide. (2022, December 23). London X London. https://www.londonxlondon.com/london-area-guides/bethnal-green/

Bethnal Green area guide—Things to do in Bethnal Green. (2017, May 3). Time Out London. https://www.timeout.com/london/things-to-do/bethnal-green-area-guide

Bianca. (2020, September 22). *Cool things to do in Chelsea.* London Kensington Guide. https://www.londonkensingtonguide.com/things-to-do-chelsea/

The Bloomsbury Hotel. (n.d.). Tripadvisor. Retrieved July 27, 2023, from https://www.tripadvisor.com/Hotel_Review-g186338-d209229-Reviews-The_Bloomsbury_Hotel-London_England.html

Breen, M. (2018, March 14). *The Duke | bars and pubs in Bloomsbury, London.* Timeout London. https://www.timeout.com/london/bars-and-pubs/the-duke-3

British culture—etiquette. (n.d.). Cultural Atlas. https://culturalatlas.sbs.com.au/british-culture/british-culture-etiquette

Brown, M. (2014, January 15). *How London got its name*. Londonist. https://londonist.com/2014/01/how-london-got-its-name

Bus leisure routes. (n.d.) Transport for London. Retrieved July 27, 2023, from https://tfl.gov.uk/travel-information/visiting-london/experience-london/bus-leisure-routes

Camden's history—Camden Council. (n.d.). Camden. https://www.camden.gov.uk/camdens-history

Canonbury. (2023, June 25). Wikipedia. https://en.wikipedia.org/wiki/Canonbury

Changing the Guard. (n.d.). The Household Division. https://www.householddivision.org.uk/changing-the-guard-overview

The Chesterfield Mayfair. (n.d.). Tripadvisor. Retrieved July 27, 2023, from https://www.tripadvisor.com/Hotel_Review-g186338-d192064-Reviews-The_Chesterfield_Mayfair-London_England.html

Chesterfield Mayfair, luxury hotel in Mayfair, London. (n.d.). Chesterfield Mayfair. Retrieved July 27, 2023, from https://chesterfieldmayfair.com/about

Christina. (2022, August 10). *How to spend three days in London: An efficient, fun-filled itinerary!* Happy to Wander. https://happytowander.com/3-day-london-itinerary/

Christmas at Kew. (n.d.). Kew. https://www.kew.org/kew-gardens/whats-on/christmas

chrysoula. (2018, December 13). *7 day London itinerary for first time visitors*. Travelpassionate.com. https://travelpassionate.com/london-itinerary-7-days/

CitizenM London Bankside. (n.d.). Tripadvisor. Retrieved July 27, 2023, from https://www.tripadvisor.com/Hotel_Review-g186338-d3199601-Reviews-CitizenM_London_Bankside-London_England.html

Comfort Inn Victoria. Tripadvisor. Retrieved July 27, 2023, from https://www.tripadvisor.co.uk/Hotel_Review-g186338-d258942-Reviews-Comfort_Inn_Victoria-London_England.html

Cooper, L. (2019, August 4). *The 10 best things to do in Tottenham*. CN

Traveller. https://www.cntraveller.com/gallery/things-to-do-tottenham

Cooper, L. (2023, March 28). *Time Out reveals the 50 best pubs in London for 2023.* Time Out London. https://www.timeout.com/london/news/time-out-reveals-the-50-best-pubs-in-london-for-2023-032823

The Corner London City. (n.d.). Tripadvisor. Retrieved July 27, 2023, from https://www.tripadvisor.com.ph/Hotel_Review-g186338-d4945399-Reviews-The_Corner_London_City-London_England.html

Crime rates in London 2023. (2023, May 17). Lodge Service. https://lodgeservice.com/crime-rates-in-london-2023/#:~: text= Overview%20of%20Crime%20in%20London%202023&text=With%20a%20total%20of%20894%2C215

Dalston. (2023, July 24). Wikipedia. https://en.wikipedia.org/wiki/Dalston#:~:text=Dalston%20began%20as%20a%20hamlet

Dalston neighbourhood guide | social. (n.d.). London on the Inside. https://londontheinside.com/map/dalston/

Dalston: The essential area guide. (n.d.). Time Out London. https://www.timeout.com/london/things-to-do/dalston-area-guide

Dean. (2019, October 15). *Dean's Verger welcomes HM the Queen with new verge.* Westminster Abbey. https://www.westminster-abbey.org/

Demography, London's population & geography. (2021). Trust for London. https://trustforlondon.org.uk/data/geography-population/#:~:text=Ethnic%20group%20populations%2C%202021%20Census

Did you know? 10 facts about St. Paul's Cathedral. (n.d.). London Pass. https://londonpass.com/en-us/blog/top-facts-about-st-pauls-cathedral

Did you know? Top facts about the Shard. (n.d.). London Pass. https://londonpass.com/en-us/blog/facts-about-the-shard

Down the pub: 10 interesting facts and figures about London pubs you might not know. (n.d.). Londontopia. Retrieved July 27, 2023, from https://londontopia.net/site-news/featured/pub-10-interesting-facts-figures-london-pubs-might-not-know/

11 interesting, fun nicknames for London. (2020, January 10). Via Travelers. https://viatravelers.com/nicknames-for-london/

11 things to do in Islington. (n.d.). London Cheapo. https://londoncheapo.com/entertainment/things-to-do-islington/

Emergency services and healthcare in London. (2019, October 17). Visit London. https://www.visitlondon.com/traveller-information/essential-information/emergency-services

FAQs: The London Bridge Experience. (n.d.). The London Pass®. Retrieved July 27, 2023, from https://londonpass.com/en-us/blog/london-bridge-experience

Fascinating Buckingham Palace facts. (n.d.). London Pass®. https://londonpass.com/en-us/blog/buckingham-palace-facts

Festival pass | VAULT festival. (n.d.). Retrieved July 26, 2023, from https://vaultfestival.com/merch/festival-pass/

The 50 best cocktail bars in London. (n.d.). Time Out London. https://www.timeout.com/london/bars/best-bars-in-london-cocktail-bars

The 50 best London attractions. (2019, April 15). Time Out London. https://www.timeout.com/london/attractions/top-london-attractions

15 interesting facts about London. (2019, April 26). Study in UK. https://www.studying-in-uk.org/15-interesting-facts-about-london/

Forge, K. (2023, April 27). *15 brilliant things to do in Battersea*. Secret London. https://secretldn.com/things-to-do-in-battersea/

4 London emergencies (and how to handle them). (2017, July 21). London Duck Tours. https://www.londonducktours.co.uk/2017/07/21/4-london-emergencies-and-how-to-handle-them/

Gay-themed walking tours. (n.d.). Visit Gay London. Retrieved July 27, 2023, from https://visitgay.london/202/gaythemed-walking-tours/

Green Rooms, London, UK. (n.d.). Booking.com. Retrieved July 27, 2023, from https://www.booking.com/hotel/gb/green-rooms.en-gb.html?aid=330631&label=msn-5sdvNGDZCacAQrfsQmG4vA-79920793889915%3Atikwd-79920789162316%3Aaud-808219487%3Aloc-188%3Aneo%3Amte%3Alp162601%3Adec%3Aqsgreen%20rooms%20hotel%20london&sid=899cbe43b311b7b9eebe74f59cc9616a&dest_id=-2601889

Guest Blogger. (2020, August 27). *The perfect 7 day London itinerary for families*. Our Globetrotters. https://www.ourglobetrotters.com/7-day-london-itinerary/

Hackney | unforgettable sport, entertainment & celebration. (n.d.). Hackney Moves. Retrieved July 26, 2023, from https://www.hackneymoves.com/

Hackney Central. (2023, July 26). Wikipedia. https://en.wikipedia.org/wiki/Hackney_Central

Heritage Victorian Hotel London—St James Court Hotel. (n.d.). St. James' Court Hotel. https://www.stjamescourthotel.co.uk/about/historyandheritage/#:~:text=St%20James%20Court%20has%20a

Highgate. (2023, July 14). Wikipedia. https://en.wikipedia.org/wiki/Highgate#History

Hilton London Bankside. (n.d.). Tripadvisor. https://www.tripadvisor.com/Hotel_Review-g186338-d8505156-Reviews-Hilton_London_Bankside-London_England.html

History. (n.d.). Columbia Road Flower Market. Retrieved July 27, 2023, from https://columbiaroad.info/history/#:~:text=The%20Flower%20market%20began%20as

History: hotels shaped by two centuries of stories. (n.d.). Imperial London. https://www.imperialhotels.co.uk/about-us/history

History and stories. (n.d.). Historic Royal Palaces. Retrieved July 27, 2023, from https://www.hrp.org.uk/tower-of-london/history-and-stories/#gs.3ax4vj

History of London - the evolution of UK's capital city. (2019). Civitatis London. https://www.londoncitybreak.com/history

Hopkins, S. (2018, September 18). *28 quirky restaurants in London for A really unique night on the town*. Secret London. https://secretldn.com/quirky-restaurants-london/

Hopkins, S. (2022, August 5). *15 of the top sports bars in London to get the drinks in this weekend*. Secret London. https://secretldn.com/sports-bars-in-london/

Hopkins, S. (2023, March 4). *10 of the very best things to do in Camberwell*. Secret London. https://secretldn.com/things-to-do-in-camberwell/

Hostelworld. (n.d.). Hostelworld. Retrieved July 27, 2023, from https://www.hostelworld.com/pwa/hosteldetails.php/Onefam-Notting-

Hill-by-Hostel-One/London/291433?source=affiliate-PHG-1100l3q6o&affiliate=PHG&ref_id=1100lwVsa7ML&utm_medium=AFFILIATE&utm_source=%20budgettraveller&uniqueclickID=1100lwVsa7ML&utm_content&from=2023-07-12&to=2023-07-13

How to watch the boat race 2023—fan parks & best spots. (n.d.). The Boat Race. Retrieved July 26, 2023, from https://www.theboatrace.org/spectator-information

Howells, T. (2016, December 14). *Island poké—Soho*. Time Out London. https://www.timeout.com/london/restaurants/island-poke-soho-1

IFS cloud cable car. (n.d.). Transport for London. https://tfl.gov.uk/modes/london-cable-car/

IFS cloud cable car fares. (n.d.). Transport for London. https://tfl.gov.uk/fares/find-fares/ifs-cloud-cable-car-fares?intcmp=54719

Insider's guide to shopping in London. (n.d.). World Travel Guide. Retrieved July 27, 2023, from https://www.worldtravelguide.net/guides/europe/united-kingdom/england/london/shopping/

James. (2014, January 2). *Epping Forest: Facts and information*. Primary Facts. https://primaryfacts.com/3404/epping-forest-facts-and-information/?utm_content=cmp-true

James, D. (2016, September 25). *10 fascinating facts about Hampton Court Palace*. Britain and Britishness. https://britainandbritishness.com/2016/09/10-fascinating-facts-about-hampton-court-palace.html

James, S. (2019, August 17). *The insider Stoke Newington neighbourhood guide*. CN Traveller. https://www.cntraveller.com/gallery/stoke-newington-neighbourhood-guide

James, S. (2023, June 9). *The best restaurants in London right now*. CN Traveller. https://www.cntraveller.com/gallery/best-restaurants-london

John Berkeley, 1st Baron Berkeley of Stratton. (2022, September 25). Wikipedia. https://en.wikipedia.org/wiki/John_Berkeley

K+K Hotel George. (n.d.). Tripadvisor. Retrieved July 27, 2023, from https://www.tripadvisor.com/Hotel_Review-g186338-d195217-Reviews-K_K_Hotel_George-London_England.html

Kaleidoscope festival. (n.d.). Kaleidoscope. Retrieved July 27, 2023, from https://kaleidoscope-festival.com/

Kendrick, A. L. (2021, November 17). *5 days in London—the perfect itinerary*. London X London. https://www.londonxlondon.com/5-days-in-london/

Kendrick, A. L. (2023, March 29). *Every Michelin Star restaurant in London 2023*. London X London. https://www.londonxlondon.com/michelin-star-restaurants-london/

Keri. (2023, May 17). *London with kids 2023: An epic five days in London itinerary your kids will love*. Bon Voyage with Kids. https://www.bonvoyagewithkids.com/five-days-in-london-itinerary/

Kind, S. (2021, April 25). *Mayfair: is this London's most elegant neighbourhood?* CN Traveller. https://www.cntraveller.com/article/mayfair-london-things-to-do

Know more about the Park Grand Paddington Court London. (n.d.). Park Grand Paddington Court London. Retrieved July 27, 2023, from https://www.parkgrandpaddingtoncourt.co.uk/we-are-the-grand-paddington-london-2144.html?gclid=Cj0KCQjwlumhBhClARIsABO6p-w_hyECNc44m-Cn4J3Axh3knq45IGktL84Ipc-xm3PBEKL9gVDscCgaAphQEALw_wcB

Lambert, T. (2021, March 14). *A history of Hampstead*. Local Histories. https://localhistories.org/a-history-of-hampstead/#:~:text=It%20takes%20its%20name%20from

LGA—Primrose Hill London. (2012). Lyndon Goode. https://www.lyndongoode.com/primrose-hill-london.html#:~:text=Primrose%20Hill%20gained%20its%20name

LGBTQIA+ guide to London. (n.d.). VisitBritain. Retrieved July 27, 2023, from https://www.visitbritain.com/en/things-to-do/lgbtqia-guide-london

Living in Bethnal Green London. (2022, December 1). Property Loop. https://www.propertyloop.co.uk/area-guides/bethnal-green-london-area-guide#:~:text=Bethnal%20Green%20was%20integrated%20into

Livingston, L. (2022, March 31). *The ultimate 5 days in London itinerary*. The Geographical Cure. https://www.thegeographicalcure.com/post/5-day-itinerary-for-london-england

The London book fair UK. (n.d.). London Book Fair. https://www.londonbookfair.co.uk/en-gb.html

The London bridge experience and London tombs. (n.d.). Viator. Retrieved July 27, 2023, from https://www.viator.com/en-GB/London-attractions/The-London-Bridge-Experience-and-London-Tombs/overview/d737-a27197

The London coffee festival 2022. (n.d.). London Coffee Festival. https://www.londoncoffeefestival.com/

London Dungeon facts for kids. (n.d.). Kiddle. Retrieved July 27, 2023, from https://kids.kiddle.co/London_Dungeon

London Eye. (2019). *The London Eye*. Londoneye.com. https://www.londoneye.com/

London fashion week—home. (2019). London Fashion Week. https://londonfashionweek.co.uk/

London for families itinerary. (n.d.). London and Partners News. Retrieved July 27, 2023, from https://media.londonandpartners.com/essential-info/london-for-families-itinerary

London itinerary 2 weeks—14 days in London vacation. (n.d.). TripHobo. Retrieved July 27, 2023, from https://www.triphobo.com/tripplans/london-itinerary-2-weeks

The London of Oscar Wilde. (2023, July 16). London Walks. https://www.walks.com/our-walks/the-london-of-oscar-wilde-tour/

London St Patrick's Day festival. (n.d.). Guide London. Retrieved July 26, 2023, from https://www.guidelondon.org.uk/events/london-st-patricks-day-festival/

London travelcard public transport pass 2019, fares & best tips. (2019). London Toolkit. https://www.londontoolkit.com/briefing/travelcard.htm

London: A history. (n.d.). History.com. https://www.history.com/topics/european-history/london-england

London's best gluten-free food | 15 great gluten-free restaurants. (2023, May 16). Time Out London. https://www.timeout.com/london/restaurants/the-best-gluten-free-restaurants-in-london

London's best cheap eats. (2023, July 20). Time Out London. https://www.timeout.com/london/food-drink/londons-best-cheap-eats

London's new year's day parade—the world's greatest street spectacular! (n.d.). https://lnydp.com/

UK survival guide. (n.d.). 1Cover Travel Insurance. Retrieved July 27, 2023, from https://www.1cover.co.nz/uk-guide/#Section5

M., Chloe. (2023, January 9). *London tourism statistics 2023—all you need to know.* GoWithGuide. https://gowithguide.com/blog/london-tourism-statistics-2023-all-you-need-to-know-5213

Mackavoy, L. (n.d.). *Queer Spaces in London.* LSE Students' Union. https://www.lsesu.com/news/article/6001/Queer-Spaces-in-London/

Mackertich, J. (n.d.). *Dalston does London proud on list of world's coolest neighbourhoods*. Time Out London. https://www.timeout.com/london/news/dalston-is-inarguably-one-of-the-worlds-coolest-neighbourhoods-100621

Make an offer on your hotel room—get A price exclusive to you. (n.d.). Justhooit.com. Retrieved July 27, 2023, from https://justhooit.com/blog/gay-hotels-london

Martin, L., Pope, N., Teasdale, C., & Collinge, M. (2022, January 21). *All the best London restaurants*. Esquire. https://www.esquire.com/uk/food-drink/restaurants/a30640079/best-restaurants-london/

Metric or imperial: What measures do Britons use? (n.d.). You Gov. https://yougov.co.uk/topics/society/articles-reports/2022/04/07/metric-or-imperial-what-measures-do-britons-use

The Montague on the Gardens. (n.d.). Tripadvisor. Retrieved July 27, 2023, from https://www.tripadvisor.com/Hotel_Review-g186338-d192036-Reviews-The_Montague_on_The_Gardens-London_England.html

The Montcalm Royal London House. (n.d.). Tripadvisor. https://www.tripadvisor.com/Hotel_Review-g186338-d10810215-Reviews-The_Montcalm_Royal_London_House-London_England.html

Museum hostel. (n.d.). Astor Hostels. Retrieved July 27, 2023, from https://astorhostels.com/hostels/museum/location/

National Theatre . (2018). Nationaltheatre.org.uk. https://www.nationaltheatre.org.uk/

Niche. (2017, May 11). Time Out London. https://www.timeout.com/london/restaurants/niche

9 secrets from Churchill War Rooms. (n.d.). Imperial War Museums. Retrieved July 27, 2023, from https://www.iwm.org.uk/history/9-

secrets-from-churchill-war-rooms#:~:text=The%20-rooms%20were%20used%20as

Nobu Hotel London Shoreditch. (n.d.). Tripadvisor. Retrieved July 27, 2023, from https://www.tripadvisor.co.uk/Hotel_Review-g186338-d12099573-Reviews-Nobu_Hotel_London_Shoreditch-London_England.html

Norah, J. & L. (2018, August 17). *3 days in London: Our perfect 3 day London itinerary*. Independent Travel Cats. https://independenttravelcats.com/3-days-in-london-itinerary/

Norah, L. (2012, April 5). *2 weeks in the UK—my perfect UK trip Itinerary*. Finding the Universe. https://www.findingtheuniverse.com/two-weeks-in-ukmy-perfect-itinerary/

North London areas & neighborhoods. (n.d.). Proficiency. Retrieved July 27, 2023, from https://www.proficiencyltd.co.uk/north-london-areas.html

Notting Hill Carnival. (2013). Notting Hill Carnival. https://nhcarnival.org/

Notting Hill history. (2017, August 30). Notting Hill Apartments Ltd. https://nottinghillapartments.com/london-notting-hill-guide/notting-hill-history/#:~:text=Notting%20Hill%20began%20its%20journey

Our history—National Theatre. (n.d.). National Theatre. https://www.nationaltheatre.org.uk/about-us/our-history/

Paddington. (2014). IMDB. https://www.imdb.com/title/tt1109624/characters/nm0924210

Park Grand Paddington Court London. (n.d.). Park Grand Paddington Court London. Retrieved July 27, 2023, from https://secure.parkgrandpaddingtoncourt.co.uk/reservation/roomdetails/?_gl=1

Parker, T. (2018, October 4). *Purezza | restaurants in Camden Town, London*. Time Out London. https://www.timeout.com/london/restaurants/purezza

Pearson, M. (n.d.). *Did you know? 10 facts about Shakespeare's Globe Theatre*. London Pass. https://londonpass.com/en-us/blog/did-you-know-10-facts-about-shakespeares-globe-theatre

Point A Hotel London Canary Wharf. (n.d.). Tripadvisor. Retrieved July 27, 2023, from https://www.tripadvisor.com/Hotel_Review-g186338-d7179933-Reviews-Point_A_Hotel_London_Canary_Wharf-London_England.html

Point A Shoreditch. (n.d.). Tripadvisor. Retrieved July 27, 2023, from https://www.tripadvisor.co.uk/Hotel_Review-g186338-d12103640-Reviews-Point_A_Shoreditch-London_England.html

Prendergast, A. (2020a, September 26). *An insider's guide to the best things to do in Battersea.* CN Traveller. https://www.cntraveller.com/article/things-to-do-in-battersea-london

Prendergast, A. (2020b, December 15). *Things to do in Brixton.* CN Traveller. https://www.cntraveller.com/gallery/things-to-do-in-brixton

Prendergast, A. & Jordan, R. (2021, January 8). *The best vegan restaurants in London.* CN Traveller. https://www.cntraveller.com/gallery/vegan-restaurants-london

The President Hotel. (n.d.). Tripadvisor. Retrieved July 27, 2023, from https://www.tripadvisor.com/Hotel_Review-g186338-d189041-Reviews-The_President_Hotel-London_England.html

Pride in London. (n.d.). Pride in London. https://prideinlondon.org/

A queer history of London—the LGBTQ+ walking tour. (n.d.). Eventbrite. Retrieved July 27, 2023, from https://www.eventbrite.co.uk/e/a-queer-history-of-london-the-lgbtq-walking-tour-tickets-160580836605

Queer London annual events calendar. (2022, June 1). Visit Gay London. https://visitgay.london/10063/queer-london-events-calendar/

Rediscover London's club scene with these top venues. (2023, February 20). Time Out London. https://www.timeout.com/london/clubs/the-best-clubs-in-london

Ridgemount Hotel. (n.d.). Tripadvisor. Retrieved July 27, 2023, from https://www.tripadvisor.com/Hotel_Review-g186338-d187680-Reviews-Ridgemount_Hotel-London_England.html

Royal Horticultural Society. (2019). *Royal Horticultural Society.* https://www.rhs.org.uk/

Royal Lancaster London. (n.d.). Tripadvisor. https://www.tripadvisor.com/Hotel_Review-g186338-d195284-Reviews-Royal_Lancaster_London-London_England.html

Salter, C. (2022, July 4). *Your ultimate London Neighborhood guide (where to live in London + map!).* Candace Abroad. https://candaceabroad.

com/london-neighborhood-guide/

Saville, A. (2022a, August 26). *Club Mexicana restaurant review*. Time Out London. https://www.timeout.com/london/restaurants/club-mexicana

Saville, A. (2022b, November 7). *Tendril review*. Time Out London. https://www.timeout.com/london/restaurants/tendril-1

Sea Containers London. (n.d.). Tripadvisor. Retrieved July 27, 2023, from https://www.tripadvisor.com/Hotel_Review-g186338-d6161763-Reviews-Sea_Containers_London-London_England.html

7 days in London: A perfect week itinerary for 2023. (2023, January 27). https://londonmymind.com/7-days-london/

Shangri-la The Shard, London. (n.d.). Tripadvisor. https://www.tripadvisor.com/Hotel_Review-g186338-d6484754-Reviews-Shangri_La_The_Shard_London-London_England.html

Shrek's Adventure general tickets. (n.d.). Shrek's Adventure! London. Retrieved July 27, 2023, from https://www.shreksadventure.com/tickets-prices/ways-to-visit/general-tickets/?

Sir John Soane's Museum. Accessed November 22, 2023. https://www.soane.org/.

16 epic things to do in Chiswick, London (2023). (2023, February 16). CK Travels. https://www.cktravels.com/things-to-do-chiswick-west-london/

Slavi. (2021, November 24). *77 astonishing quotes about London (perfect for Instagram)*. Global Castaway. https://globalcastaway.com/quotes-about-london/

Soho. (n.d.). Tripadvisor. https://www.tripadvisor.co.uk/Attraction_Review-g186338-d187582-Reviews-Soho-London_England.html

St. Ermin's Hotel, autograph collection. (n.d.). Tripadvisor. https://www.tripadvisor.com/Hotel_Review-g186338-d248802-Reviews-St_Ermin_s_Hotel_Autograph_Collection-London_England.html

St. James' Court, a Taj hotel. (n.d.). Tripadvisor. https://www.tripadvisor.com/Hotel_Review-g186338-d265539-Reviews-St_James_Court_A_Taj_Hotel-London_England.html

Stanners, L. (2019, October 17). *The ultimate guide to Hampstead*. CN Traveller. https://www.cntraveller.com/gallery/things-to-do-in-hampstead

Stanners, L. (2020, September 19). *Highgate: The insider's guide.* CN Traveller. https://www.cntraveller.com/gallery/highgate-london-insider-guide

State opening of Parliament. (2019). UK Parliament. https://www.parliament.uk/about/how/occasions/stateopening/

The story of Hampton Court Palace. (n.d.). Historic Royal Palaces. Retrieved July 27, 2023, from https://www.hrp.org.uk/hampton-court-palace/history-and-stories/the-story-of-hampton-court-palace/#gs.3avssp

The 10 best things to do near K+K hotel George, London. (n.d.). Tripadvisor. Retrieved July 27, 2023, from https://www.tripadvisor.co.uk/AttractionsNear-g186338-d195217-K_K_Hotel_George-London_England.html

10 facts about London Stadium. (2022, March 16). TFC Stadiums. https://tfcstadiums.com/10-facts-about-london-stadium/

Ten LGBTQ+ spots to visit in London. (2021, May 27). Time Out London. https://www.timeout.com/london/things-to-do/ten-lgbtq-spots-to-visit-in-london

10 things you didn't know about Kensington Palace. (n.d.). Gem Hotels. Retrieved July 27, 2023, from https://www.gemhotels.com/blogs/10-facts-about-kensington-palace

These are the best times to visit London. (2015). US News.com. https://travel.usnews.com/London_England/When_to_Visit/

Things to do in Soho. (n.d.). Visitlondon.com. https://www.visitlondon.com/things-to-do/london-areas/soho

Things you might not know about the borough of Islington. (2017, January 31). Londonist. https://londonist.com/london/features/islington-facts

3-Day London itinerary—72 hours in London. (n.d.). London City Break. Retrieved July 27, 2023, from https://www.londoncitybreak.com/london-in-three-days

Tickets and prices. (n.d.). Historic Royal Palaces. Retrieved July 27, 2023, from https://www.hrp.org.uk/hampton-court-palace/visit/tickets-and-prices/#gs.3avl7e

Time zone & clock changes in London, England, United Kingdom. (n.d.). Timeanddate. Retrieved July 27, 2023, from https://www.timeand

date.com/time/zone/uk/london#:~:text=Time%20Changes%20in%20London%20Over%20the%20Years%20

Top facts you should know about Tower Bridge. (n.d.). Tower Bridge. https://www.towerbridge.org.uk/top-facts-you-should-know-about-tower-bridge

Top ten house clubs in London. (n.d.). London Sound Academy. https://www.londonsoundacademy.com/blog/top-ten-house-clubs-in-london

The top 10 London city tours (w/prices). (n.d.). Viator. Retrieved July 27, 2023, from https://www.viator.com/London-tours/City-Tours/d737-g12-c5330

The Tophams Hotel . Tripadvisor. Retrieved July 27, 2023, from https://www.tripadvisor.co.uk/Hotel_Review-g186338-d209138-Reviews-The_Tophams_Hotel-London_England.html#MAPVIEW

Tottenham. (2020, February 24). Wikipedia. https://en.wikipedia.org/wiki/Tottenham

Travelodge London city hotel. (n.d.). Tripadvisor. https://www.tripadvisor.com/Hotel_Review-g186338-d13569031-Reviews-Travelodge_London_City_hotel-London_England.html

Travelodge. (n.d.). Tripadvisor. Retrieved July 27, 2023, from https://www.tripadvisor.com/Hotel_Review-g186338-d193057-Reviews-Travelodge_London_Covent_Garden-London_England.html

Trooping the Colour. (n.d.). Www.trooping-The-Colour.co.uk. Retrieved July 27, 2023, from http://www.trooping-the-colour.co.uk/

21 top sites in London for history lovers—context travel. (n.d.). Context Travel. https://www.contexttravel.com/blog/articles/21-top-sites-in-london-for-history-lovers

22 things to do in Shepherd's Bush by a local (2023). (2023, April 22). CK Travels. https://www.cktravels.com/things-to-do-shepherds-bush-london/

2023 what's on—the London coffee festival 2023. (n.d.). London Coffee Festival. Retrieved July 26, 2023, from https://www.londoncoffeefestival.com/Whats-On

2 weeks in London: The ultimate itinerary for 13–14 days. (2022, January 17). https://londonmymind.com/2-weeks-london/

The ultimate LGBTQ guide to London. (n.d.-a). Matador Network. Retrieved July 27, 2023, from https://matadornetwork.com/read/lgbtq-guide-london/

The ultimate neighbourhood guide to Camden Town London. (n.d.). Retrieved July 27, 2023, from https://goodmigrations.com/city-guides/london/camden-town/

Underbelly festival—earls court and cavendish square. (n.d.). Underbelly. Retrieved July 27, 2023, from https://www.underbellyfestival.com/

Visit. (n.d.). Shakespeare's Globe. Retrieved July 27, 2023, from https://www.shakespearesglobe.com/visit/?gclid=EAIaIQobChMIkvPovfqagAMVQ6jVCh0J2QeVEAAYASACEgI7AfD_BwE

W., Beatrice. (2022, May 22). *Top 10 sensational facts about Greenwich Park London.* Discover Walks Blog. https://www.discoverwalks.com/blog/london/top-10-sensational-facts-about-greenwich-park-london/

Warner Bros. Studio Tour tickets. (n.d.). Warner Bros. Studio Tour London. https://www.wbstudiotour.co.uk/tickets/

Wembley Stadium. (n.d.). Wembley Stadium. https://www.wembleystadium.com/

Where to go. (n.d.). Lord Mayors Show. https://lordmayorsshow.london/practicalities/where-to-go

Wikeley, R. (2019, October 26). *Canonbury: the insider guide.* CN Traveller. https://www.cntraveller.com/gallery/canonbury

Wikipedia Contributors. (2019a, April 24). *London.* Wikipedia; Wikimedia Foundation. https://en.wikipedia.org/wiki/London

Wikipedia Contributors. (2019b, April 29). *History of London.* Wikipedia; Wikimedia Foundation. https://en.wikipedia.org/wiki/History_of_London

Wikipedia Contributors. (2019c, July 30). *London Government act 1963.* Wikipedia; Wikimedia Foundation. https://en.wikipedia.org/wiki/London_Government_Act_1963

Wikipedia Contributors. (2023a, April 19). *History of Shepherd's Bush.* Wikipedia; Wikimedia Foundation. https://en.wikipedia.org/wiki/History_of_Shepherd%27s_Bush#:~:text=Shepherd%27s%20Bush%20is%20a%20neighbourhood

Wikipedia Contributors. (2023b, June 15). *London's New Year's Day Parade*. Wikipedia; Wikimedia Foundation. https://en.wikipedia.org/wiki/London%27s_New_Year%27s_Day_Parade#:~:text=The%20London%20parade%20is%20the

Wilkinson, C. (2022, June 28). *Tofu Vegan restaurant review: plant-based Sichuan sizzlers*. Time ut London. https://www.timeout.com/london/restaurants/tofu-vegan

IMAGE REFERENCES

alfcermed. (20th October 2016). *London Covent Garden Urban* [image]. https://pixabay.com/photos/london-covent-garden-urban-landscape-1750934/

anizzz32. (13th September 2019). *Notting Hill London, UK* [image]. https://pixabay.com/photos/notting-hill-london-uk-house-urban-4470322/

davidkenny91. (29th November 2017). *Wimbledon Final Tennis Centre* [image]. https://pixabay.com/photos/wimbledon-final-tennis-centre-court-2983451/

designerpoint. (5th August 2016). *London, Britain, Eye* [image]. https://pixabay.com/photos/london-britain-london-eye-sky-1572444/

djblackerry. (6th April 2020). *United kingdom, London, Changing of the guard* [image]. www.pixabay.com. https://pixabay.com/photos/united-kingdom-london5004636/

5477687. (7th June 2017). *Portobello Road, London Market* [image]. https://pixabay.com/photos/portobello-road-london-market-2377084/

khfalk. (6th February 2017). *Street Art, London, Shoreditch* [image]. https://pixabay.com/photos/street-art-london-shoreditch-2044085/

12019. (12th June 2017). *Big Ben, Bridge, City* [image]. https://pixabay.com/photos/big-ben-bridge-city-sunrise-river-2393098/

12019. (10th June 2013). *Boats, River, Bridge* [image]. https://pixabay.com/photos/boats-river-bridge-buildings-123778/

London-Reference -England. *London Map* [image] https://gisgeography.com/london-map-england/

Pfuderi. (19th April 2017). *Pub, Bar, Drink* [image]. https://pixabay.com/photos/pub-bar-drink-london-tap-beer-2243488/

Pfuderi. (26th April 2017). *London Bus, St Pauls* [image]. https://pixabay.com/photos/london-bus-st-pauls-2254133/

pierre9x6. (14th June 2020). *London, Sunset, England* [image]. https://pixabay.com/photos/london-sunset-england-architecture-5297395/

PublicCo. (5th April 2017). *National History Museum London* [image]. https://pixabay.com/photos/natural-history-museum-london-2203648/

PublicDomainPictures. (13th December 2010). *Britain, England, English* [image]. https://pixabay.com/photos/britain-england-english-london-2938/

PublicDomainPictures. (13th December 2010). *Westminster Palace* [image]. https://pixabay.com/photos/westminster-palace-building-night-2892/

StockSnap. (5th September 2015). *Picadilly Circus, People, Crowd* [image]. https://pixabay.com/photos/piccadilly-circus-people-crowd-busy-926802/

tonysell. (10th February 2020). *Transport, Subway, Architecture* [image]. https://pixabay.com/photos/transport-subway-architecture-4834813/

VIVIANE6276. (13th December 2018). *Camden Town District, London* [image]. https://pixabay.com/photos/camden-town-district-london-england-3872368/

Vicjo. (18th September 2022). *Autumn, City* [image]. https://pixabay.com/photos/autumn-city-london-england-7460414/

waldiwkl. (26th May 2014). *Tower Of London* [image]. https://pixabay.com/photos/tower-of-london-london-london-bridge-353868/

Printed in Great Britain
by Amazon

d2de6b2d-5ca5-4753-a898-7b6ea7854331R01